SACRED EARTH
CELEBRATIONS
A SOURCEBOOK

Written and Illustrated
by Glennie Kindred

PERMANENT PUBLICATIONS

Published by
Permanent Publications
Hyden House Ltd
The Sustainability Centre
East Meon
Hampshire GU32 1HR
United Kingdom
Tel: 0844 846 846 4824 (local rate UK only)
         or +44 (0)1730 823 311
Fax: 01730 823 322
Email: enquiries@permaculture.co.uk
Web: www.permanentpublications.co.uk

Distributed in the USA by
Chelsea Green Publishing Company, PO Box 428, White River Junction, VT 05001
www.chelseagreen.com

Front cover painting by Glennie Kindred
Cover design by Sarah Howerd

Design and typeset by Sarah Howerd, www.sideways14.co.uk

Printed in the UK by CPI Antony Rowe, Chippenham, Wiltshire

All paper from FSC certified mixed sources

The Forest Stewardship Council (FSC) is a non-profit international
organisation established to promote the responsible management of
the world's forests. Products carrying the FSC label are independently
certified to assure consumers that they come from forests that are
managed to meet the social, economic and ecological needs of present
and future generations.

FSC
www.fsc.org
MIX
Paper from
responsible sources
FSC® C005094

British Library Cataloguing-in-Publication Data
A catalogue record for this book is available from the British Library

ISBN 978 1 85623 175 6

Disclaimer: The author and the publisher cannot be held responsible for accidents or any harm
caused due to using any of the craft project ideas or herbal remedies contained in this book.

*This book is dedicated to the Earth
and all those who walk the path of Love.*

CONTENTS

By celebrating the Earth's cycles
we empower ourselves in new
and inspiring ways.

We are free to follow
our own path,
to trust in our
inherent intuitive abilities
and our integrity.
This leads us to rediscover
the sacred in ourselves
and all that
surrounds us.

We live within a
unified whole and
we do nothing in isolation.

Every single thing we do which is life-
affirming, aids the process of healing
ourselves, each other and the Earth.

Blessed Be

PREFACE

THIS IS A NEW EDITION of the much-loved old favourite, *Sacred Celebrations*, and contains a lot of new material as well as new artwork. It has been many years since its first publication in 2000, and as a direct result of following the Celtic festivals, how I relate to the Earth has deepened and changed during that time. There are many subtle shifts in my understanding, which the re-writing of this new edition has given me the opportunity to integrate.

We are now at a time of increasing climate chaos and global change. We are becoming more aware of our impact on the planet and our influence on her delicately balanced ecosystems. Never before have we needed so desperately to change our thinking patterns, from seeing ourselves as separate from the Earth and each other, to seeing ourselves as part of a vast interconnected network of life.

Celebrating the Earth and her cycles helps us to re-find our path to a more respectful relationship with the whole of life on Earth. These festivals are part of a living tradition. They link us to our Celtic ancestors who had a deep respect for the Earth. Each festival helps us to discover more about ourselves and our intrinsic connection to her. And, like all of life on Earth, these festivals are evolving. Celebrating them today, we are free from any hierarchy, superstitions, and fears, fixed systems or rules that may have come with celebrating them in the past. We are free to celebrate them in whatever way we choose. We can celebrate with others or alone. We can make up our own ceremonies and explore our honest and authentic selves. They bring an exciting edge to our lives as we intuitively re-form them into something new and yet connected, something that belongs to our own times and helps us to explore our own evolving relationship with the Earth and deepen our inherent personal spirituality.

Celebrating the Earth Festivals gives us a greater awareness of ourselves and the journey we are on. As we embrace the understanding that our lives are intrinsically interwoven with the Earth's, a new and subtle shift begins to take place in our consciousness. Love and unity become our strength and our guide, and from this perspective our own healing and the healing of the Earth are one.

With Love ♡

glennie Kindred) 2014

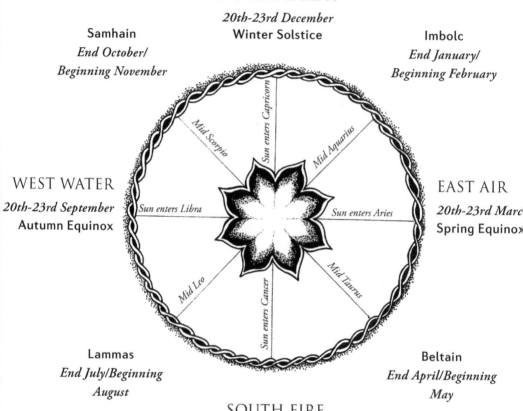

NORTH EARTH

20th-23rd December
Winter Solstice

Samhain
End October/
Beginning November

Imbolc
End January/
Beginning February

WEST WATER

20th-23rd September
Autumn Equinox

EAST AIR

20th-23rd Marc
Spring Equinox

Mid Scorpio

Sun enters Capricorn

Mid Aquarius

Sun enters Libra

Sun enters Aries

Mid Leo

Sun enters Cancer

Mid Taurus

Lammas
End July/Beginning
August

Beltain
End April/Beginning
May

SOUTH FIRE

20th-23rd June
Summer Solstice

THE WHEEL
OF THE YEAR

To celebrate the Earth's yearly cycle is to take part in an ancient tradition that has been handed down to us since before Celtic times. The old Celtic festivals fall at eight points during the year, and are a means by which we can connect to the Earth's passing seasons and acknowledge the way this resonates within ourselves, as part of the natural world.

THROUGHOUT THE BOOK I use the word 'Celtic' as a term which recognises this as a cultural lineage in the lands of England, Wales, Scotland and Ireland, as well as all over Northern and Western Europe. Many of their traditions have been lost, destroyed by the Christian church that sought to establish a new patriarchal god, and destroy the worship of Pagan gods and goddesses. Much can be rediscovered through folk customs, legends and folktales. Much has been kept alive through Pagan tradition, druidic and bardic lore and Pictish and Celtic art. The Christian calendar, on close examination, overlaid its own festivals to fall at the same time as the Celtic ones, but with a subtle difference of perspective. This was necessary, as part of the conversion process, which changed the whole spiritual experience of the people of these lands. The church also taught us to view spirit and matter as separate realms, and to fear the inner worlds, our intuition and the dark. This is so deeply entrenched, that even those without any religious belief are deeply influenced by it. We also feel ourselves to be separate from and superior to the rest of nature, and that men are superior to women. This fragmented state has brought great damage to the Earth's environment and to us.

In order to change this perspective, there is a need to see ourselves and our relationship to the Earth, the Moon, the Sun and each other with new eyes. We need to re-learn what we have forgotten and re-find connections long buried or suppressed. We have been conditioned for so long to only use our logical intellectual minds; it is important that we begin to become aware of and listen to our intuitive side. It is our conferred power and inherited right, and without this balance we are incomplete as human beings.

Following the Wheel of the Year and the Earth festivals has no hierarchy of spiritual authority. We are each able to follow our own path, to break free of outworn attitudes, damaging dogma and concepts, and to transform and change as we listen to our inner voice and seek our higher visions. They help us to learn to be part of the natural world again and feel ourselves to be part of creation and not somehow fragmented and separated. Everyone and everything is sacred. Everything is connected. Every thought, and everything we say or do creates a resonance and a reaction within us and all around us. We do nothing in isolation.

Celebrating the Earth festivals brings a structure to our lives by consciously making a connection to the passage of time and our path within it. This helps us to remember to honour and celebrate the Earth and her seasons, ourselves and each other, our achievements as well as our losses. We can come together as a community, to share food and drink, to dance, sing, reflect and share our experiences and understanding. Or we can use this time to be on our own, to spend some time in sacred space or set off on a pilgrimage, to reflect and explore our relationship with the Earth and our evolving inner understanding. It is a gift we can give ourselves every six weeks, which brings us more stability, balance and connectedness.

Each festival is celebrated with a different focus according to the prevailing season and the season yet to come. But celebrating the Wheel of the Year is not just a matter of changing from one season to the next. Beneath the manifestation of seasonal change, there is also change within the subtle energies of the Earth. These energy patterns affect us all (consciously or unconsciously) so that by understanding the flow and direction of this energy, we can move with it, as true inhabitants of our planet Earth: belonging, part of and flowing with it on all levels of our being.

The Eightfold sub-division of the year is marked by the four fixed points in the year forming a cross. These are called the Quarter Points and are the Winter Solstice (20th-23rd December), the shortest day and the longest night; the Summer Solstice (20th-23rd June) the longest day and shortest night; the Spring Equinox (20th-23rd March), and the Autumn Equinox (20th-23rd September), both of which are when day and night are of equal length. These are fixed points in the year: the exact day and time each year can be found in any good diary. (See Recommended Reading page 234.)

These Four Quarter Points are then crossed again by what are known as the Cross Quarter Festivals. These are the four great fire festivals of our Celtic past. They fall at the seasonal peaks and are used to celebrate and participate with the power of nature. They are the point at which we can connect with the developing energy of the new season ahead.

Imbolc or Imolg is celebrated at the end of January/beginning of February, when winter has reached its peak and the first signs of spring are showing themselves. Beltain is celebrated at the end of April/beginning of May when spring has reached its peak and summer is becoming apparent. Lammas or Lughnasad is celebrated at the end of July/beginning of August, when summer has reached its peak and the first signs of autumn are showing. Finally, Samhain is celebrated at the end of October/beginning of November, when autumn has reached its peak, and winter is beginning to feel that it has arrived.

THE QUARTER POINTS

The Solstices

The great cosmic clock of the waxing and waning cycle of the Sun reaches its peak at each of the Solstices. Solstice means 'the standing of the Sun' (Latin). From Winter Solstice to Summer Solstice the Sun's influence is waxing, reaching its peak at the Summer Solstice, the longest day and shortest night. From Summer Solstice to Winter Solstice, the Sun's influence is waning and the darkness reaches its peak at the shortest day and longest night of the Winter Solstice.

The Solstices then are a time to stop, and to look back on where the half-yearly cycle has brought you; a chance to look forward and see the direction in which the next half-yearly cycle may lead you; a moment to be conscious of your life's flow and direction; a time to express your hopes and fears, your intentions; to assimilate your learning and celebrate your achievements; a time to celebrate the light; a time to celebrate the dark; a moment to be conscious of the way this waxing and waning of the Sun affects our lives, and to celebrate this influence and what it means to us.

When the light is increasing from Winter Solstice to Summer Solstice, all beings are influenced by the increase in light, expressing their own identity and uniqueness, expanding outwards into the material world, becoming more individual and independent. But as the light is decreasing from Summer Solstice to Winter Solstice, nature and life as a whole is expanding inwards, reflecting, becoming more intuitive, tapping into their inner wisdom.

The Equinoxes

At the Spring and Autumn Equinoxes, day and night are of equal length all over the world. The focus here is the balance of light and dark, the outer world balanced by the inner world. Both are equal.

The Equinoxes fall at the beginning of the seasonal changes: spring with its promise of summer, and autumn with its promise of winter. The new season will affect all of life and bring changes within as well as without, as well as releasing new energy patterns. Times of transition are often chaotic and stressful, but out of this chaos, new ways, new ideas and new directions can manifest. The Equinoxes are a time to take action, transform, release the past, and move forwards. Use these points as a focus for the direction you wish to go in. This means you will meet the new energy poised and prepared.

THE CROSS QUARTER POINTS

THE QUARTER POINTS OF the Winter and Summer Solstices, and the Spring and Autumn Equinoxes, are then crossed again by the Cross Quarter Points, known in the past as the Four Great Fire Festivals. These may have been celebrated in the past by lighting big fires on the hilltops, uniting communities by a common bond of celebration. These four Cross Quarter festivals fall at the seasonal peaks, at the point when the season is about to change into the next, and this is the best time to use this developing energy. Because of this, their application during the year's cycle is of deepest and significant importance to us if we wish to work with the Earth's energies, and participate in a process of positive change both for the Earth and ourselves.

Each of the Cross Quarter festivals offers a unique opportunity for us to celebrate and be aware of the developing energy and what this could mean for us, to bring about manifestation through the power of our deepest wishes and positive intent.

IMBOLC is at the end of January/beginning of February. Winter is at its peak, but the days are lengthening slightly, and the first signs of spring are apparent. The active phase of life is beginning as the Sun's power returns. Our intuitive receptive energy is strong at this time and it is the right time to bring out what has been assimilated and understood on the inner levels during the winter months. It is a time for new beginnings, emerging ideas and the outer growth of personal seeds from their incubation period within.

BELTAIN is at the end of April/beginning of May. Spring is at its peak, the days are getting longer and warmer, and the first signs of summer are establishing themselves. The Earth's energies are at their most active now and bring an increase in manifestation and fertility. This is a time when the life force is at its most potent and powerful, and the right time to use this expansive energy to its fullest potential.

LAMMAS is at the end of July/beginning of August. Summer is at its peak, but the days are beginning to shorten slightly and the first of the harvest, the grain, is being gathered in. Here we can begin to assimilate and gather in our own personal harvest, the manifestation of our heart's desires, and the fruits of our active labour. It is a time to take a reflective look at ourselves and return to the spiritual inner world for deeper understanding of our actions.

SAMHAIN is at the end of October/beginning of November. Autumn has reached its peak now, the harvest is all gathered in. The days are getting shorter and winter is

almost upon us. We return once again to the reflective spiritual realms inside ourselves, for regeneration of the Spirit, rest, and contact with our inner wisdom.

Each of these Cross Quarter festivals is influenced by one of the four elements through the four fixed astrological signs. The fixed signs are very energetic. Their energy endures, and they propel projects to completion. Imbolc falls in the middle of Aquarius, an Air sign; Beltain falls in the middle of Taurus, an Earth sign; Lammas falls in the middle of Leo, a Fire sign; and Samhain falls in the middle of Scorpio, a Water sign.

There are some who like to fix these Cross Quarter festivals by dates on the calendar: Imbolc eve on 2nd February, Beltain eve on 30th April, Lammas eve on 2nd August, and Samhain eve on 31st October. I prefer to look at the position of the Moon and any other astrological information, and choose a time when these and other influences are at their most potent. Each year the weather is different and the seasonal shifts are a subtle reflection of this. I also prefer to put aside some time when the moment feels right for me. This is a spontaneous thing. I walk the land, sit with trees, collect herbs, muse, write and experience the moment.

Celebrating the Cross Quarter Points may go on for several days. It is entirely up to you. There is no one telling you what to do or how to do it, just your own intuition and desire to align your life's journey closer to the Earth

THE MOON

The Moon and Her Cycles

The Earth revolves around her axis in one day. The Moon orbits around the Earth in approximately 29 days (a lunar month). The Earth orbits around the Sun in one year. These cycles are the alternating waxing and waning rhythms of Gaia. Understanding their influence and becoming more aware of how their energy affects our lives, enables us to be integrated into their cosmic dance.

As seen from the Earth, the Moon and the Sun appear to be equal in size. The Sun is 400 times larger than the Moon, but it is also 400 times further away from the Earth. At New and Full Moon, the Earth, Moon and Sun are aligned. When the Sun and Moon are diametrically opposite each other, the Moon is full. When the Sun and Moon lie in the same direction, the Moon is new.

The Sun and the Moon influence the energy cycles of all life on Earth. The Sun gives us light and warmth in an outward dynamic of manifest energy. The Moon's reflective qualities distribute this energy during the hours of darkness, bringing receptivity and assimilation.

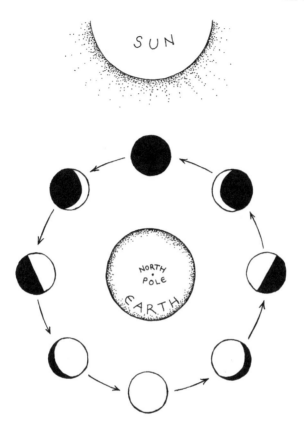

The celebration of the eight Celtic festivals provides a connection to each phase of the solar year and its season. Within that framework the Moon interweaves its monthly lunar cycle. The Winter and Summer Solstices and the Spring and Autumn Equinoxes are fixed astronomical points in the solar year. Using an astrological diary, you can check the influence the Moon will bring to these celebrations. (See Recommended Reading page 234.)

The four great fire festivals of Imbolc, Beltain, Lammas and Samhain, are not fixed points and can be celebrated when the Moon's influence most complements the energy of the festival.

The influence of the Moon was recognised and honoured by the earliest people, who noticed that the approximate 29-day cycle of the Moon's phases corresponded to women's menstrual cycles. The Moon became feminine and was personified as the Triple Moon Goddess whose unfolding cyclic phases from new to full to dark was understood as part of the cosmology and pattern of the web of life and death, representing the three great cycles of birth, maturity, death and rebirth. The Moon's aspects were personified as the Maid, emerging New Moon Goddess; the Mother, abundant provider and Full Moon Goddess; and the Crone, wise woman, guardian of the inner realms, the Dark Moon Goddess.

The Moon is the closest celestial body to the Earth and its force of gravity is so powerful, it pulls on the oceans, causing two high tides a day. This same influence affects all the fluids on the Earth, including the underground waters, the circulation of our body fluids, the ovulation cycle, the growth patterns of plants, and the migration patterns of birds.

The Moon also influences the watery nature of our unconsciousness, our emotions, our moods, feelings and perceptions. She is reflector and shadow, and the cycles of her three aspects influence us more deeply than most of us are aware. Keep a Moon diary and watch how closely your patterns are connected to the Moon's outward and inward flow. The alternating waxing and waning of the Moon's cycles when understood, can enhance and balance the way we choose to live our lives.

THE PHASES OF THE MOON

New Moon

The Sun and the Moon rise together in the East. The Moon is invisible because it is hidden by the Sun's brightness. The New Moon is sacred to the Maid aspect of the Triple Moon Goddess, bringing inspiration and intuition. It is like a new seed, full of potential and energy. This is the time for new beginnings, the time to begin new projects, take new directions, make new resolutions. It is the best time for invocation and speaking out your intent. The New Moon rises at sunrise and sets at sunset.

Waxing Crescent Moon

The Moon rises mid morning and sets after sunset. She can be seen in the western sky in the late afternoon. The rising waxing energy of the Moon brings growth to all ideas and plans. In nature, foliage, fruit and seeds develop when the Moon is waxing.

Waxing Half Moon (First Quarter)

The Moon rises about midday and sets about midnight. She can be seen from soon after she rises until she sets. This is a period of growth and activity on all levels.

Gibbous Moon

Visible soon after she rises just before sunset, to when she sets just before dawn. From here to Full Moon, make the most of her abundant waxing energy. It is a time of activity and expressing yourself through your feelings.

Full Moon

Rising at sunset and setting at sunrise the Moon is visible throughout the night. The Sun and Moon are opposite each other in the sky and the Moon is reflecting all of the Sun's light. This is the time for celebration and outward expression. It brings change, revelation and emotional peaks. Sacred to the Mother aspect of the Triple Moon Goddess, it brings abundance and the blending of Spirit and Matter. This is the peak of psychic power and heightened energy, sometimes causing us to feel unbalanced and crazy (lunatic). This is the time of culmination, fruition, and completion. The Moon is so bright she can light the night and cast Moon shadows. This brings a period of increased light that is sufficient to assist photosynthesis in plants, and thereby increases growth.

Disseminating Moon (Waning Full Moon)

The Moon now begins to wane. She rises mid-evening and sets mid-morning (one hour later after sunset each night). The waning Moon brings self-assessment, looking within, and reflection. In nature, the waning Moon cycle promotes root development. She is visible from the time she rises until she sets.

Waning Half Moon (Last Quarter)

The Moon rises around midnight and sets around mid-day, and is visible from when she rises to when she sets. The Moon continues to wane, bringing inner reflection, transformation and change.

Balsamic Moon (Waning Crescent Moon)

The Moon rises before dawn and sets mid-afternoon. This is the very last sliver of Moon seen in the eastern sky in the early morning. The waning Moon is sacred to the Crone or wise woman aspect of the Triple Moon Goddess, bringing inner wisdom and entry into the dark inner mysteries and knowledge. This is the time for banishing rituals, to let go of things no longer helpful to you, to break psychic links.

The Dark of the Moon
The Moon is said to be dark for three days before the New Moon when it has waned so far that it is no longer visible in the sky. The Dark Moon brings a deeper understanding of our journey and guidance from within. It is a time for quiet inward reflection, assimilation, for learning from our experience, and preparing for the new cycle by seeking out new intentions to take you forward.

THE MOON AND THE ASTROLOGICAL SUN-SIGNS

THE MOON PASSES THROUGH a different Sun-sign every two and a half days. When she reaches the astrological sign the Sun is in, it is the New Moon. At the Full Moon, she is in the opposite astrological sign from the Sun. By integrating both the outward manifest qualities of the Sun-sign, and the inward reflective qualities of the Moon's cycle we gain a deeper understanding of ourselves and these unseen influences. An astrological diary will give you daily information of the influence of the Moon and other planets (See *Earth Pathways Diary* page 233). A more detailed understanding of the way the Moon influences us, can be gained by consulting an astrologer.

Moon Qualities
The Moon brings us closer to our emotions and feelings and influences our receptive nature, helping us to assimilate our experiences, adapt and change and to nurture others and ourselves. We are more likely to sense what's going on rather than to consciously know. She brings us intuition and reflections from within.

Moon in Aries ☾ ♈
Aries will act directly and instantly, a natural starting point for new projects and plans. It is the right time to channel all that 'me-first' energy to initiate change, and to act on impulse. Ruled by Mars and the element of Fire, it brings assertiveness and courage to express your feelings. Be aware of selfishness and impatience.

Moon in Taurus ☾ ♉
When the Moon is in this fixed Earth sign, a calm stability will settle around you. Ruled by Venus, you feel sensuous, secure, solid, unhurried and earthed. You may also feel possessive and stubborn.

Moon in Gemini ☽ ♊

Gemini Moon brings stimulation and activity, spontaneity, communication, conversation and a myriad of interesting ideas and connections. Gemini is a mutable Air sign ruled by Mercury. Moon in Gemini is the time for communicating your feelings, and making connections within and without. It may bring great restlessness and scattered emotions.

Moon in Cancer ☽ ♋

This Water sign is ruled by the Moon herself. This is a highly emotional time when tears can come readily and there is a tendency to become over-sensitive, dependent and needy. Memories are strong, and the home, family and mothering are important. It is a good time to look after family and friends, to make time for your home, and to nurture yourself.

Moon in Leo ☽ ♌

This fixed Fire sign, ruled by the Sun, demands attention on all levels. It is a time for magnanimous gestures and creative celebrations. Be generous with your feelings and your enthusiasm in sensitive and thoughtful ways.

Moon in Virgo ☽ ♍

Virgo, mutable Earth sign, ruled by Mercury, asks us to look at what needs to be taken care of. Moon in Virgo is the patterning seer, arranging, categorising and tending, until every meticulous detail has been integrated and understood. There may be a tendency to lose the overview and become over-critical of yourself or others.

Moon in Libra ☽ ♎

A harmonious and romantic phase for family, friends and lovers to relax and appreciate each other. Libra is an Air sign, ruled by Venus, and will restore balance to the emotions through diplomacy and the refining of ideas and ideals. Use this time for making things beautiful and harmonious. You may be indecisive and extremist.

Moon in Scorpio ☽ ♏

Scorpio is a fixed Water sign ruled by Pluto and Mars. When the Moon passes through this sign, feelings are intense and deeply felt, sometimes to the point of obsession. During this time you delve into your unconscious and come face to face with the dark shadowy side of yourself. You may have to look at your fears and find the courage to deal with the emotions this brings up.

Moon in Sagittarius ☽ ♐

This Fire sign brings optimism and a relaxed easy-going phase. Ruled by the benevolent Jupiter, the Moon in Sagittarius connects us to our inner wisdom and prophetic truths, allows us to be spontaneous and to seek adventurous solutions. It can be a restless time bringing a need to throw off all responsibility.

Moon in Capricorn ☽ ♑

This Earth sign is ruled by Saturn, the great teacher, and will bring strength and wisdom, as well as a desire to organise yourself, and set down some rules and guidelines. Find ways to help yourself deal with your emotions, but avoid becoming too pessimistic or rigid.

Moon in Aquarius ☽ ♒

An Air sign ruled by Uranus, the Aquarian Moon brings a love of personal freedom and individuality. There is an ability to detach yourself from old emotional patterns. This Moon encourages us to be idealistic, challenging, unpredictable, and to reveal hidden truths.

Moon in Pisces ☽ ♓

This Water sign, ruled by Neptune, will bring dreamtime into your waking life, and magic into all possibilities. Moon in Pisces will bring intuition and receptivity, and a place from which to wish all your dreams into reality. Spiritual awareness and meditation are the highest use of these energies. Celebrate the irrational and the Spirit paths; leave the rational mind behind.

Remember to also weave in the direction in which the Moon **is moving.** Keeping track of this brings a connection to the natural energy flow and this means you can make the best use of the Moon's phases in your daily life.

Learn where the Moon rises and sets in relation to your house and at different parts of the cycle. Step outside more often at night, when the Moon is full and the land is brightened by her light, and also when the night is dark, letting your eyes adjust, finding your night vision and letting your instincts grow.

CELEBRATION, CEREMONY AND RITUAL

The way you celebrate the Celtic festivals is a matter of choice and experiment. What matters most is the experience of communicating with the outer world, bursting with created abundance, and connecting to your inner levels and spiritual path. The changing year provides a wealth of experiences through the cyclic ebb and flow of the Sun's energy. Interwoven with this, are the monthly cycles of the waxing and waning Moon, and the planetary influences.

Each festival is a chance to feel yourself as part of the whole, and also to connect to the moment, the here and now. From this point of being you can look back on what you have been doing, feeling, thinking, on your health, and on your spiritual journey. You can also look forward with an understanding of the Earth's (and your) inherent energy flow, to where you wish to go, how you may best use the oncoming energy for your greater good, the greater good of the Earth, and all those around you.

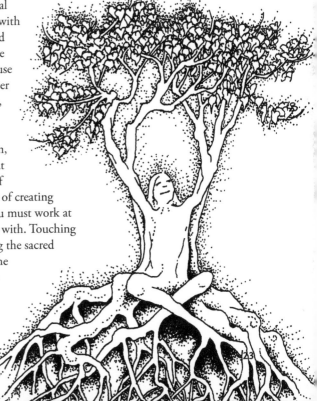

It may be that you wish to celebrate these festivals on your own, or with a close friend; it may be that you prefer to gather with a group of friends and explore the possibilities of creating ceremonies and rituals together. You must work at the level you feel most comfortable with. Touching your deepest feelings and expressing the sacred will bring with it a connection to the inner core of your being. If you are celebrating with friends, you will inevitably become closer as a result of this sharing.

THE FIVE ELEMENTS

CENTRAL TO ANY CEREMONY or sacred space are the four directions and their corresponding four elements of Air, Fire, Water and Earth. The fifth element, Spirit or Ether, is the invisible force that is everywhere and nowhere, within and without. It is both immanence and transcendence, interwoven in all life. When creating a sacred circle to include all the elements, Spirit or Ether's place is at the centre, and also around the circumference. On the pentacle, Spirit is the top point with the four elements making up the other points. The four quarters, four elements and four directions create the symbol of the equal armed cross. Spirit surrounds it and is represented by a circle. This makes a cross within a circle, a symbol that pre-dates Christianity.

The Five Elements can be used to create a temporary or permanent sacred space. This may be done in a room, a garden, on a hilltop, amongst a group of trees, or anywhere that feels special to you.

You may wish to create a space that is large enough to include a group of friends taking part in group celebrations. If you have a large garden or a piece of land you could create five permanent shrines to each of the elements, to visit and work with throughout the year. If you have a spare room or attic which can be used as sacred space, it is a wonderful asset and can be used for group meetings, meditation, healing, and any time you need to connect deeply to your inner world.

At its most simple, place something in each direction to represent each element. This brings focus to each element and creates a sacred circle. Alternatively, create elemental hangings to hang on the wall using coloured wool or painted material, or a painting that summons the power of each element visually. Decorate five sticks with coloured wools and threads, hang things from them to suggest that element, and place these in each of the directions. You may make five shrines, one for each element, placing appropriate things in each. The seasonal changes bring fresh things to add and new understanding. Honour Spirit, at the centre and the circumference. This may include flowers, candles or a beautiful chalice.

You may want to celebrate on your own, and therefore need only a small space. The elements can be laid out on a round tray or beautiful wooden board kept for this purpose.

Using a standard compass, turn it until the red arrow is on North. This fixes the position of the four directions. Central to creating sacred space and using the five elements is visualisation. You must visualise each element strongly in your mind's eye in order for their energy and power to become manifest. Speak words that strengthen their connection to you. By doing this, you are creating links and connectors for energy and understanding to flow through.

Earth in the North

Earth is rooting and grounding, anchoring us to this body and this life, and for this reason I like to honour and thank her first, but the choice is yours. Place a stone, a crystal or seasonal flowers in the North to represent the Earth. Visualise the material world: trees, plants, rocks, soil, animals and insects. Visualise the mountains and the caves, the roots, the minerals and crystals beneath the surface of the Earth. The North is the place of our inner wisdom and ancient knowledge. Earth brings containment, fertility, abundance and experience. Give thanks to the Earth for its supportive and nurturing energy, for the season and for your life.

Air in the East

Air is a unifying and connecting force, which we all breathe in and which gives us life. It is continually flowing and it is through Air that we send our words and the vibrations of our thoughts and intentions, our power to communicate. Place a feather, a nest of eggs, a bell, or chime in the East. East is the place of the rising Sun, a new day, new beginnings. Visualise the wind, the flow and patterns that air creates; the sky with the birds gliding and travelling along the air currents; gales and strong winds, gentle balmy winds; visualise sounds travelling, your voice and the power of our words, the power of song, music and your breath. Use your voice to sing or speak out an acknowledgement, and welcome the gifts of Air. Give thanks for clean Air and for each breath you take.

Fire in the South

Fire consumes, transforms and cleanses. It can be creative or destructive. Fire is an active force, bringing change. It is the spark of our vital energy, passion, creativity, spontaneity, sexuality and our active imaginations. Light a candle in the South, or burn some incense or native herbs. Its colours are red, orange and gold. Give thanks for the heat of the mid-day Sun, fire at the heart of the home, warmth in the winter, cooking fires. Give thanks for the active vitality of the spirit of Fire, for our will power, the power of intention, the energetic creative force that brings change and transformation.

Water in the West

Place a bowl of spring water in the West, the place of the setting Sun, reflection of our unconscious, our intuition and the world within. Give thanks for the life-giving element of Water, for without it we cannot live. Give thanks for the sea, the rhythm of the waves, the Moon, springs bubbling from the Earth, flowing streams, mighty rivers, waterfalls, rain, tears. Water connects us to our emotions, the pull of our hearts, our deepest feelings, through which we learn the power of love, compassion, and receptivity to the great mysteries of life.

Spirit

Place a beautiful bowl or chalice at the centre of your circle to represent the fifth element, Spirit. Give thanks for the uniting force that cannot be seen, cannot be named, and yet is all around us, connecting us to all that is, above and below, within and without and at the centre of our being and our spiritual path. Spirit is the unseen world, unformed and unknowable, other dimensional possibilities. It is always with us, connecting us to the great unity of life. It is universal energy and the transformative power of Universal Love. It is what has been and what will be and yet it is always only in the present moment.

Welcome your spirit guides, your inner guardians; welcome the spirits of the place; welcome the spirits of the ancestors and the descendants; welcome the nature spirits, the plant and tree devas, the faerie and other elementals; and welcome the spirit of the season, and what this means to you.

Creating Outdoor Shrines and Sacred Space

With each season you will find new ways of representing the Five Elements, and each season presents a new opportunity to creatively express each of them. This is the most powerful way of understanding how these forces work within us. The enjoyment is in the active involvement of creating a sacred shrine area. It is a connecting and stilling process through which balance and inner harmony are achieved.

Creating an impermanent outside sacred space is much the same as creating one within a room, but outside things need to be visually stronger and simpler. A large stick put in the ground at each of the four directions, with coloured ribbons is a quick and effective way of marking the directions if a large group of friends are gathering. Always use natural materials, gathered with consideration and care. Use sticks, leaves, white stones, bark mulch or strips of coloured material to create a sacred circle on the ground. At dusk light your space with night-lights in jam jars.

If you want to be more ambitious, make a large hoop (one metre in diameter or less) from a freshly cut hazel rod (approx. five foot long). Bind the ends together with string and then, using material and paint or wool and threads, create a sacred hoop or shield for each of the directions. This can then be brought out and hung up in the appropriate direction, inside or outside. The Spirit shield can be hung in a tree or from the ceiling. (See page 96 for how to make a sacred shield.)

Semi-Permanent Shrines for the Five Elements

Freshly cut hazel rods can be used to create outside areas, arches or bowers where each of the elements may be represented. They are not completely permanent, but they will last for a few years before the wood eventually becomes brittle.

Four rods create a much stronger archway than two. Make four holes in the ground with a metal spike and embed the thick end of four freshly cut hazel rods into the ground. Cross them over in the middle and tie them together with strong string. This creates an area where you can add things to suggest each of the elements. You may wish to have them high enough to hang an elemental shield in, or much lower and more enclosed, where candles can be lit. The bower can be decorated with greenery, flowers, grasses, twigs, woven with willow, and hung with relevant items. Each new season brings different things to decorate them with - these may not be permanent either. Coloured wool, material and threads quickly fade in the sun and the rain.

Earth in the North
Wrap weaving plants, such as honeysuckle, ivy or willow whips, around the hazel. Weave in any flowers of the season, wheat or grasses. Decorate with wool or coloured threads of Earth colours: greens and browns or gold according to the season. Bring in potted plants, trees or herbs (wrap the pots in coloured material). Add crystals, rocks, bones, pieces of wood, bowls of fruit, nuts, leaves, flowers or other gifts from the Earth.

Air in the East
Its colours are white, pale purples and pale yellow. Wrap the hazel rods in thin gauzy material, net or strands of coloured wool. Wind chimes may be hung up inside. Tie on feathers and streamers of wool and threads to catch the breezes. Thin silvery things are good. A nest with eggs (stone or chocolate) represents new beginnings and a spiral pattern represents the flow and eddies of air currents.

Fire in the South

Use materials, ribbons, scarves and wool of oranges, red and golden yellows. Shiny gold materials catch the light. Light candles, burn incense and herbs. Representations of the Sun may be hung in the middle or round the edge. Bring in red, orange and yellow flowers.

Water in the West

Wrap blue, green and purple ribbons and wool around the hazel rods. Hang painted fish made out of salt dough or felt, hang shells and use shells for making patterns on the ground. Make a pond in a large bowl at the centre or a special drinking bowl of spring water. Glass bowls let in the light from both the Sun and the Moon, but need to be kept clean.

Spirit at the Centre

Create a mandala using natural materials, beginning with a flat round stone, a round of wood, or something similar at the centre. Radiate the pattern out from the centre using leaves, stones, flowers, earth, and any available material. Each of the elements can be represented here as a focus for the whole. Circle the whole thing with night lights and another at the centre. Or place a beautiful empty bowl or chalice at the centre, or some flowers or living twigs of the season. Anything you wish to bring focus to, give thanks for, or honour can be placed at the centre. This can include photographs, or anything that has significance and brings connection.

Permanent Shrines for the Five Elements

If you wish to create a permanent place in your garden or on your land for the Five Elements, you will need to use materials that will endure. Material and wool quickly lose their colours and eventually rot but can be replaced at each festival to keep the energy fresh and connected. Rock, stone and well-oiled wood may be used; plants which are permanently growing there, or in pots, especially herbs, are good. Many herbs and trees have traditional associations with the Five Elements and the Celtic festivals. (See charts on pages 30-34.)

Anything made from fired clay is another permanent and natural material. It will get dirty in the wind and the rain, but can be washed easily enough. Other less durable items can be added to your outside areas at the time of the celebration, and taken inside afterwards.

Working with and understanding the Five Elements brings a connection to the Earth and all its aspects. These elemental energies are to be found within ourselves and within our lives. They can be consciously worked with, like any other system. Choose an element to work with when their qualities are uppermost at a particular time of the year, or because you feel you need to connect and communicate with that particular energy at any given time.

Once you have set up the directions and elements, energetically visualise an energy field around the outside of your space. Burn incense or herbs, state your intent and ask for protection or the presence of your guardian spirits and guides. The words you use are a personal choice, reaching out or reaching in. The important thing is that they make a connection that brings a change within your consciousness. Words are power. Use them wisely. Only say what rings true.

EARTH

*The North * Midnight * Midwinter Solstice*

*The Gift of Life * Fertility * The Physical World*
*The Force of Gravity * The Life Force * The Uniting Force*

*Consolidation * Nurturing * Sustaining * Regenerating*
*Abundance * Growth * Supportive * Healing*
*The Web of Life * The Wisdom of Experience*
*Expansion * Rooting * Darkness*

*Mountains * Soil * Rocks * Stones*
*Crystals * Minerals * Medicines*
*Trees * Plants * Herbs * Flowers * Seeds*
*Animals * Insects * Food*
*Bones * The Ancestors*

*Mother Earth * Gaia * The Green Man*
*The Triple Goddess * The Underworld*
*Nature Spirits * Faerie * The Sidhe*
*Barrows * Burial Mounds * Standing Stones*
*Dragons * Dragon Paths * Leylines*

*Taurus * Virgo * Capricorn * Saturn*

The Power of Union, Fertility, and Manifestation

Tarot ~ Pentacles

*Black * Greens * Browns*

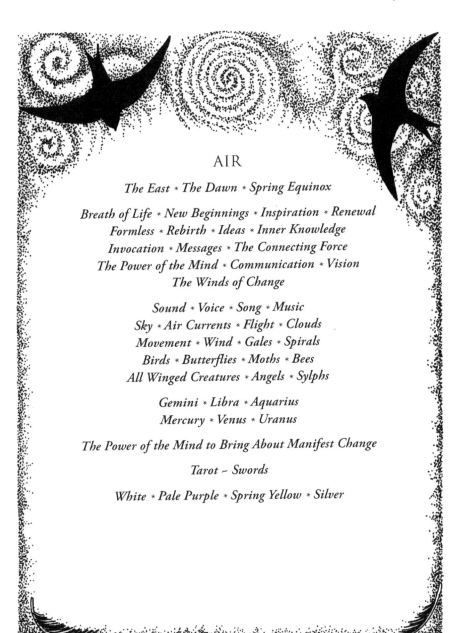

AIR

*The East * The Dawn * Spring Equinox*

*Breath of Life * New Beginnings * Inspiration * Renewal*
*Formless * Rebirth * Ideas * Inner Knowledge*
*Invocation * Messages * The Connecting Force*
*The Power of the Mind * Communication * Vision*
The Winds of Change

*Sound * Voice * Song * Music*
*Sky * Air Currents * Flight * Clouds*
*Movement * Wind * Gales * Spirals*
*Birds * Butterflies * Moths * Bees*
*All Winged Creatures * Angels * Sylphs*

*Gemini * Libra * Aquarius*
*Mercury * Venus * Uranus*

The Power of the Mind to Bring About Manifest Change

Tarot ~ Swords

*White * Pale Purple * Spring Yellow * Silver*

FIRE

*The South * Midday * Midsummer Solstice*

*Activating * Transformative * A Catalyst*
*The Will * Creativity * Energising * Change*

*All Consuming * Cleansing * Purifying * The Imagination*
*Power * Expansion * Destruction*
*Consuming * Courage * Passion*
*Vibrant * Sexuality * Spontaneity * Inspiration*
Burning Away the Old or the Past

*The Hearth Fire * Wild Fire*
*Flames * Glowing * Smouldering * Roaring*
*Light * Sunlight * Starlight * Our Inner Fire*

*The Serpent * The Salamander * The Phoenix*
Fire Dragons

*Jupiter * Mars * the Sun*
*Sagittarius * Aries * Leo*

The Power of Active Energy to Bring About Transformation

Tarot ~ Wands

*Red * Orange * Yellow * Gold*

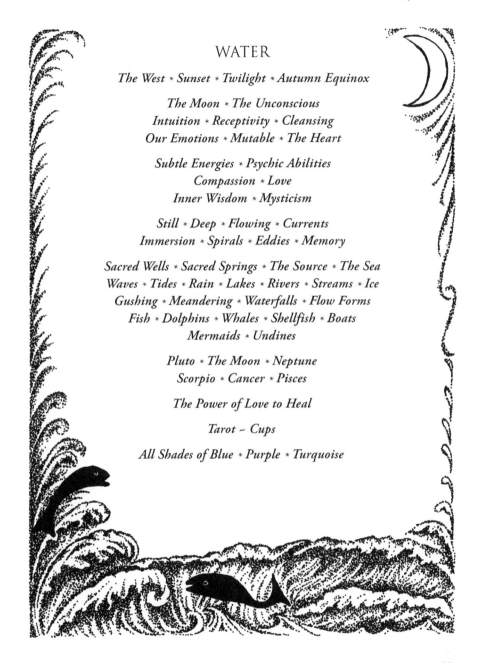

WATER

*The West * Sunset * Twilight * Autumn Equinox*

*The Moon * The Unconscious*
*Intuition * Receptivity * Cleansing*
*Our Emotions * Mutable * The Heart*

*Subtle Energies * Psychic Abilities*
*Compassion * Love*
*Inner Wisdom * Mysticism*

*Still * Deep * Flowing * Currents*
*Immersion * Spirals * Eddies * Memory*

*Sacred Wells * Sacred Springs * The Source * The Sea*
*Waves * Tides * Rain * Lakes * Rivers * Streams * Ice*
*Gushing * Meandering * Waterfalls * Flow Forms*
*Fish * Dolphins * Whales * Shellfish * Boats*
*Mermaids * Undines*

*Pluto * The Moon * Neptune*
*Scorpio * Cancer * Pisces*

The Power of Love to Heal

Tarot ~ Cups

*All Shades of Blue * Purple * Turquoise*

SPIRIT

The Fifth Element

Quintessence

The Centre of the Circle
and the Circumference

Unity

Ether

The Web of Life

Essence of All Things

Inclusive

The Source

Eternal

Ever Present

Connecting Force

The Limitless Is

Unconditional Love

Universal Love

Within and Without

Infinite Love

Timelessness

Omnipresent

All Encompassing

Oneness

MANIFESTATION THROUGH THE FIVE ELEMENTS

ALL PHYSICAL MATTER IS ALIVE with vibrational energy and we, as part of that energy, interact with the flow and direction it takes, setting energy in motion with our emotions, thoughts, words, intentions and actions. We bring fertility, transformation and new possibilities to each and every moment, whether we are conscious of it or not.

Each of the Five Elements, both within us and in the physical world around us, can be used as a dynamic energy system that we can consciously work with to influence what we create for ourselves and for the world.

Fire

Fire is energy and action, our conscious choice to set energy in motion. We can harness our willpower and set clear intentions to initiate change in our lives and in the world. We always have choice and can decide where we want to put our 'Yes!' Fire is expansion, transformation, action and a catalyst for change. Fire is the spark of the imagination, the spark of inspiration, both of which come from within us. Fire is the boldness to begin, the initiator, intention, the transference of what is inside us into outer action.

Water

Water is the element of our inner world, our feelings and unconscious longings, which influence our thoughts and actions. Water is healthy when it is flowing. As it swirls and eddies it becomes self cleaning, self regulating and self revitalising. We too are healthy when our watery emotional energy is flowing. E-Motion = Energy in Motion. This is achieved by releasing and sharing our emotions, and by letting go of old negative and unwanted emotional patterns. When we generate the flow of positive, life enhancing emotions such as loving kindness and appreciation, we not only send this out to others but it becomes who we are and what we attract towards ourselves.

Air

Air is the connecting force, uniting us with all of life here on the Earth. Air is the element of communication and the mind. Our thoughts and words are constantly creating waves of vibration which travel through the intricate Web of Life, creating change and manifestation in so many unseen and undreamed of ways. Life is a circulating interconnected energy flow. Whatever thoughts and words we send out, return to us, so that we truly become what we think. If we believe in a positive outcome, then we are already united with it, removing the separation created by doubt. Thus we hold the key to our own future, by the beliefs we set in motion in the present.

Earth

Earth is the element of the physical world and is where everything eventually becomes manifest. Through Earth we are connected to the Matrix (from the Latin 'Mater', meaning 'Mother', 'Womb', 'Creatress', 'Mother of Life'), the unity, the interconnected web of all life. This fertile force, of which we are a part of, is creating and regenerating life continuously. This is the web of all possibilities, the circuit of interconnected energy from which all matter takes form. From the hidden world within us, we create the seeds of life, bringing our inner world of thoughts, beliefs and feelings into manifestation through the uniting and infinitely fertile Web of Life.

Spirit

Spirit is the force that unites all the actions of the elements together, so that there is no separation, only a fusion of dynamic union that is our continuous relationship to the present moment. Spirit is the quintessential energy of life, the all-inclusive open circuit of energy, with no beginning and no end; endless streams of all possibilities; continuous creation in the making. Each moment is potential waiting to happen. Our consciousness stabilises these waves of possibility. We create what we bring into being with every thought, emotion and action and thus we are our own creation.

This endless process is continuously happening, whether we are conscious of it or not. By choosing to be aware of this alchemy, we can use the Five Elements to enhance what we bring into being and what seeds we make fertile (Earth); to affirm new thinking patterns and belief systems based on love and trust (Air); to generate unconditional love, healing and happiness in our lives and in the world (Water); to set in motion our most positive intentions (Fire); and to develop unity consciousness through our conscious connection to the Web of Life and the potential held in each moment (Spirit).

MEDITATION

MEDITATION IS AN ANCIENT TECHNIQUE and one that is important to master. It is based on the mind's ability to stay concentrated upon one single focus in a poised and relaxed manner. The mind is then able to make a shift in consciousness from this single focus to a place of peaceful stillness. The benefits of meditation go way beyond the time spent in actual meditation, bringing greater relaxation and tranquillity, improved concentration, and more control over the thought processes. It also brings improvement in memory, improvement in creative thinking, enhances self-understanding and aids spiritual development.

Meditation is a huge subject in itself and there are many different techniques. Buddha, one of the earliest recorded meditation teachers, taught his followers to concentrate on their breath and made it clear that all benefits of concentration can be gained from this method alone. This is therefore a very good starting point.

To begin, your body needs to feel relaxed. There are many variations, but sitting with a straight back helps our lungs to open fully. Consciously explore your body from your head to your toes, checking all parts are without tension. Generally, people's awareness is centred too high. Relax and sink. Feel your roots going down into the Earth and let the Earth's energy flow through you.

Begin to focus on your in and out-breath from the nose, but do not let your attention follow the breath into the lungs. Feel the cool air on the in-breath, and the warm air on the out-breath. Awareness should always remain at the nostrils. Inevitably, thoughts will come crowding in, but look upon them as people trying to distract you. Each time you find your mind has drifted away from your breath, just gently bring your focus back to your breathing.

A mantra, which is a word or phrase, is another focus for meditation. Choose any positive affirmation you feel is helpful to you. Say it quietly on the out-breath or the in-breath. Eventually do not say it out loud at all, but only in your mind. Each time you find yourself following your thoughts, come back to your point of concentration. Thus the mind circles round and round a key point or idea, and in the process, will bore a 'well' down through layers of thoughts, until a breakthrough is made onto another level.

With practice you will be able to hold an image strongly in your mind without the interference of unwanted thoughts. This is essential for all shamanic work involving visualisation, for inner journeys and many healing techniques.

CREATING A CEREMONY

OBSERVING THE EIGHT CELTIC FESTIVALS creates an opportunity for participation in a continuous on-going cyclic process where we can consciously become connected to our own and the Earth's energy. Through them we can touch our innermost feelings and awareness and this allows us to express the sacred in our lives.

If these ceremonies are to be effective and powerful, they must help us find the source of our personal power, a deeper awareness of the underlying life force, the power of unconditional love and a deeper relationship with the Earth.

A ceremony will touch us deeply when it brings the spiritual and physical worlds into balance. It need not be complicated. In fact, the simplest things work the best as they can be interpreted on many different levels by everyone.

In my experience, a bit of pre-planning and a few special things gathered together before a ceremony will help to make it both meaningful and special. Before you begin, go out into nature, even if it is only into your garden, take a moment to find your own stillness and connect to the Earth of which you are a part. Breathe deeply and connect to each of the elements around you. Gather some flowers or sprigs of different leaves. Even in the depths of winter; there are twigs with buds forming, and evergreens to gather.

Creating a seasonal shrine is a lovely thing to do and helps make your connection to the Earth's cycle stronger. Using a compass, stand at the centre and find the four directions. Place something in each direction to represent its related element. Mark an outer circle by laying out stones, grasses, twigs, flowers, petals, herbs or strips of material or scarves and light candles all around. Speak out any invocations of intent as you do these things to help focus the energy of your celebration and your circle.

Bring together the things you will use to represent the Five Elements: a crystal or stone for Earth; a feather or chime for Air; a candle or incense for Fire; a special bowl of spring water for Water; something for the centre to represent Spirit, such as a chalice or beautiful bowl. This is part of the build-up to the actual celebration and connects you to your innermost sacred world. Go for a walk if you can. Really feel the moment within the Earth and within yourself. Perhaps a tune or chant will come to you as you make your preparations.

Make time for meditation before you start so that you are open to your intuition and free from mental clutter.

Get some food and drink together beforehand, ready for the end of the ceremony. Food is always good to 'ground' the experience and creates a time for journalling if alone or socialising if with friends. Bless the food and drink and eat as part of the celebration. Simple homemade seasonal food is always best.

Celebrating With Friends

If you are celebrating with a group of people, it is good to take it in turns to choose the venue, decide how to represent the Five Elements, plan the flow and content of the ceremony, and let the rest of the group know the time, place and any special things to bring. In this way the ceremonies are varied, and everyone gets a chance to be creative working together. This leaves the rest of the group to be completely free to get totally involved in the ceremony. There should be at least two people who are 'holding' the energy of the ceremony, who know what's going to happen next, and keep it flowing. Ask everyone to bring food and drink to share, and something for the shrine. Decorations, incense, candles, greenery, flowers, all help to add atmosphere to the moment. It is good to dress up and make the moment special, even if it is only by wrapping a coloured scarf around your waist, hair or shoulders.

When planning a ceremony, take into account the season, the venue, its size, whether it is indoors or outdoors, whether there is room to dance. Is it all right to make a lot of noise like drumming? How can you help everyone to get the most out of it? How can you engage and include the children? How will you give thanks for the Five Elements? How will you bring the group together to begin the celebration? What activities will you do once you have created sacred space? How will you close it?

Opening a Ceremony

Bring everyone together for the opening ceremony and to create sacred space together. This helps us to anchor our selves in the moment and facilitates a shift in atmosphere. If you are celebrating in a group, the opening ceremony should unite the whole group together. Drumming together will immediately invoke a sense of ceremony and let everyone know it is about to begin. Holding hands in a circle completes a circuit of energy. Sing a chant together, tone notes, anything which helps create a mesmerising trance-like atmosphere. If you are on your own, bring yourself into the present moment, drum, chant or tone. After this initial shift, settle your energy through meditation and grounding, and coming into the stillness of the moment.

The opening ceremony helps us to focus on our intention. What we bring, through the power of our intent, will reverberate through all we do and say. It helps us feel the power of the life force within ourselves, to feel the presence of the spirit world so close to ours; to feel alive... and in the moment!

Acknowledge, give thanks and welcome each of the Five Elements and the directions in turn. Then welcome in your spirit guides and helpers, the ancestors, the descendants, the nature spirits, the spirits of the place and the spirit of the season or festival.

I particularly like creating ceremonies that give the whole group the greatest freedom of expression, and a chance for everyone to share themselves and speak from the heart. For example when thanking the Five Elements, encourage the whole group to speak out and create their connection, as they feel moved to. It doesn't matter if things get repeated or if people speak at the same time. Everyone makes the connection for themselves and for others. Someone may plan a group activity for each element. Alternatively, five people may be chosen to represent and speak for each element. It is always better to speak from the heart and not to read something. Trust that the right words will come... they always do! If you are celebrating alone or with a small experienced group, the whole thing can flow spontaneously.

The Middle of a Ceremony

Once you have created this heart-filled or sacred space there are many choices as to what could happen next. You may have a 'check in' – taking a moment to think about or journal to understand how you feel in this moment. If you are in a group, have a 'go-round' to share these thoughts with each other. Often a common thread emerges and evolves from the 'check in'. You can also make a plan before the celebration or have a specific intention you wish to explore or anchor.

Closing a Ceremony

At the end of the celebration, it is equally important to have a closing ceremony. Bring the group back together by drumming, making a circle, holding hands again. If you are on your own, come back to your centre again. Thank each element in turn; thank all your spirit guides, guardians and helpers for their help and involvement in your celebration. Thank the elemental beings of the Earth who, unseen to you, may have drawn nearer. Thank the ancestors. Thank each other. Appreciation lifts the spirits and opens the heart.

You might end on a chant or a free-flow of words or sound, Om, originally Sanskrit but now adopted in western circles to mean 'Spirit in All Things'; Awen, originally welsh for inspiration and the muse, and now used by Druids and Pagans to mean 'Flowing Spirit of Life'.

End on a Cone of Power. This is made by toning any of the vowel sounds. Begin with a whisper and gradually build up to a peak of energy and sound. Picture all the good work of the ceremony filling your inner being and spreading out into your life and into the world to make a difference. Then bring the energy back down to the Earth, anchoring it in the Earth as you bring the sounds or words back to a whisper. Hold the sweet silence at the end for a while.

CHILDREN

IT IS VERY IMPORTANT that our children learn to acknowledge and express their inner world, to balance the over-emphasis in our society and their education on material achievements and status. Taking part in ceremonies will help them to make connections to the natural world and to their creative and intuitive processes, as well as giving them an opportunity to explore their subconscious and their imaginations.
It is a time for parents and children to be together, for people without children to get to know friends' children, for relaxing and playing together, to talk about belief systems, and the understanding of life's mysteries. It is an opportunity for all ages to come together and learn from each other. It can be helpful for children approaching puberty to be welcomed into the adult world. Young girls are welcomed into womanhood as they begin menstruating, and young boys are able to take their place amongst the men. This is the old tribal way and there is much value to be gained from it.

If you are celebrating with a group of friends, there are often children of different ages. This, of course, makes it hard to involve all of the children all of the time. It is better that they can engage in what interests them, and be free to disengage if it doesn't. This respects their freedom to do only what they want to do. It is equally important that the children respect the activities of the rest of the group. For example: not running around and making a lot of noise where people are meditating, and not disrupting a ceremony.

Often children will want to be involved in only some parts of the celebration, such as drumming or singing and chanting, or dancing. Lighting the candles and incense, collecting greenery and flowers, making a special nature shrine, are all activities which children love to join in with. It makes them feel a part of it right from the beginning. Children learn best from adults who talk to them as if they matter. Children will become involved if that is the group's intent, and their opinions, choices and needs are listened to within the context of the opinions, choices and needs of the rest of the group.

Children's imaginations are very vivid. They like to take the initiative and be active. With this in mind, it is not hard to help them become involved. Stories are a wonderful way of bringing them together. Telling and re-telling the myths and legends and folk stories of our lands are wonderful for the whole group, as well as the children. Story time, with mugs of cocoa around the campfire, is an enjoyment for all ages, a chance to snuggle up together and gaze into the fire.

Most children love to perform and, with the help of sensitive adults, they can be encouraged to put on plays or dance performances that explore the theme of the festival being celebrated. Rehearsing can absorb them totally while the rest of the group is involved in a quieter activity which may not interest them.

Craft Activities

A craft activity at each celebration usually appeals to children and adults alike. It creates another opportunity to be pleasurably involved together and for shared discussions. Making things which are relevant to the season, using natural materials as far as possible, is as liberating an experience for the adults as it is enjoyable for the children.

The choice of activity and where it will happen requires some consideration. Often it is easier to work on the floor inside or outside. Put an old sheet or blanket down first. This can be gathered up at the end, keeping all the mess in one place. Use masking tape or string or glue sticks, and avoid using pots of glue or paints that may be tipped over. If these are to be used, it is better to have them on a separate table covered in newspaper or plastic sheeting. The adults can then keep an eye on it and any spills can easily be cleaned up if accidents happen.

A set of acrylic paints in tubes is a great asset as small amounts can be squirted out at a time. They are water-soluble and yet once dry, will not smudge or come off. They dry quickly, can be used thickly or thinly (mix with water), and work well on all kinds of different materials. It is also worth investing in a few good paintbrushes for careful work as well as some cheaper ones for the younger children. If some different materials need to be bought for a special activity, most people are happy to pay a share of the costs, and you can check this beforehand.

Modelling natural clay is a potent and powerful medium that spans all age groups and abilities. Children abandon themselves to it, forming and re-forming it in a timeless primal transformative process which spans back over the aeons. It is wonderfully pleasurable and deeply absorbing even if the finished model isn't kept and the clay is squidged back into a ball. It doesn't require any special skills although, of course, skills will be learnt.

Put a piece of plastic sheet or plastic tablecloth down first. Sharpened sticks make good modelling tools. Wooden boards or cardboard pieces are ideal for putting your models on while you work, and stops the models sticking to the plastic. If you want to join two pieces of clay together, roughen both surfaces and press them together. Try to avoid using water. It's a lovely sensation when clay gets really wet and slippery, but models will disintegrate and your work area will get really messy. Partly dried-out clay (it is called 'cheese-hard') is wonderfully easy to carve with a vegetable knife.

It is possible to buy small bags of clay through a craft supplier, or ask your local potter or school to sell you some. It's very cheap. Once opened, keep the clay wrapped up in a damp cloth and wrap the whole thing in plastic. It will keep for years like this. Any dried clay can be wrapped up separately from the main piece in a wet rag (cotton T-shirt material is best), and then wrapped in a plastic bag. In less than a week it will be soft enough to squeeze back into a usable lump again.

A BOX OF USEFUL ART AND CRAFT MATERIALS MAY BE GATHERED TOGETHER providing a basis for the art and craft activities. A small amount of money from the group members could set this up, and then sharing in the cost of new materials when needed.

The box should include:

* *A few pairs of child-friendly but sharp scissors (round-ended)*
* *A pot of felt-tip pens*
* *A pot of pencil crayons, a box of wax crayons*
* *Acrylic paints in tubes*
* *Glue sticks, PVA glue, tubes of Copydex*
* *Masking tape, Sellotape*
* *Paintbrushes/different sizes and types*
* *Coloured wools and natural sheep's wool*
* *Embroidery threads/silks*
* *Cardboard*
* *Coloured sugar paper, white drawing paper*
* *Tissue paper, crepe paper*
* *Leather, leather thong, chamois leather*
* *Ribbon, scraps of material*
* *Needles for sewing, bodkins for wool*
* *String*
* *Sticks of all sizes from cocktail sticks to natural sticks and twigs*
* *Driftwood*
* *Seed cases*
* *Beads*
* *Shells*
* *Feathers*
* *Dried flowers*
* *Basket maker's willow*

Plus many other natural materials. All can be used in many different creative ways.

One of the main problems with clay is that the models become brittle as soon as they dry out. They need to be fired, which effects a chemical reaction and hardens the clay. Nowadays this is done in a kiln, but in the past clay was hardened in an earth kiln. If you are having an outdoor fire as part of your ceremony, you can dry the models out on the edge of the fire, (not too close and not in the fire or they will explode) or in the sunshine. When the models are dried out properly put them in an old biscuit tin (make sure it is tin, including the lid) and place this right on the edge of the fire, turning the tin frequently, being careful to use thick oven gloves. At the end of the evening, pile the hot ashes around and on top of the tin, and leave until morning. This is a very simple way of firing clay, but it works sufficiently well to be able to harden the models. They can then be painted with acrylics or rubbed with shoe or furniture polish for an interesting natural effect.

Other modelling materials can be used which will dry hard in the air or can be baked in an ordinary oven. None of them have that raw earthiness or tactile quality of natural clay, but they are still fun to use and easily bought or made. Making your own modelling material is easy and inexpensive. I include here a couple of my favourite recipes:

Salt Dough

300g (10oz) plain flour

300g (10oz) salt

1 tbsp oil

Approx 200ml (6.7 fl. oz) water

Mix ingredients together in a bowl. Add more water if necessary. Turn onto floured board and knead. It is better if made the day before and keeps well in the fridge in a plastic bag. Knead in food dye to colour or glaze with egg before baking. Make sure everything is dried out completely before baking or cracking will occur. Bake for 20 minutes on gas Mark 4 or 160 degrees Celsius. Too hot an oven will also cause cracking.

Play Dough

2 tsp cream of tartar

1 cup plain flour

Half cup salt

1 tsp vegetable oil

1 cup water

Mix in a bowl to form a smooth paste. Mix in food dye to colour. Mix everything together and cook the mixture in a non-stick saucepan. Cook slowly stirring all the time until the mixture eventually forms a stiff ball. Stop cooking at this point and knead the ball as it cools on a wooden board, for at least 5 minutes. Stored in an airtight container, it will last several months. If you wish to bake items hard, dry out well first, then bake in a medium-hot oven for 15-20 minutes. Can be painted and varnished afterwards.

Guided Visualisation/Inner Journeys

Guided visualisation journeys are a great favourite with children of all ages. Let them choose a crystal to hold, and have some light blankets or scarves for them to lie on, or put over themselves. Cushions help them to be comfortable. Begin by asking them to focus on their breathing and then tell them you are going to help them go on a journey in their minds. The nature of the journey may be worked out beforehand. It may be into a garden, or through the woods, through a hole in a tree; it may be out into space; it may be flying on the back of a bird, or a mythical animal, or under the sea, or a journey to meet their animal guide or helper. The possibilities are endless. Speak slowly; leave plenty of space for their minds to fill in the details. In fact, it is important not to put too much detail in, and to encourage them to look around them in their mind's eye. It is especially important with younger children to make short journeys (about five minutes), and leave plenty of time for hearing all about what happened to them, what they saw, and how they felt on their journey. This sharing is a very pleasurable part of the experience and they look forward to telling the rest of the group what they saw and where they went. Drawings or paintings can be made of a special part of the journey that they wish to remember.

Forums and Games

Different members of the group may have skills and knowledge that they can share with the children. There could also be time put aside for a special focus (a forum) in which the whole group is invited to share and discuss what they know on a given subject. Subjects could include: the Moon, stone circles, labyrinths, Earth energy, leylines, crop circles, the chakras, the aura, crystals, astrology, the green man, herb lore, tree lore, animal symbolism, and many more related subjects. The children will choose subjects that they wish to discuss. The introduction of a talking stick may be used sometimes. This is a stick that is handed round the group. The person holding the stick is the only person who should be speaking at any one time.

Games are also a good way to involve children. There are many new non-competitive games that can be played and shared with the whole group, providing fun and interaction on many levels. Be inventive and creative, make up new games that can become favourites; encourage the children to make up games; encourage the adults to join in and abandon themselves to their child within.

Creating Shrines

Creating a special area using natural materials is a wonderful activity to do with children. Provide them with willow whips, stones, shells, flowers, leaves, seeds etc. Even grass cuttings can be arranged to form patterns. Every environment will bring new materials. The patterns may be random or you can suggest a basic shape such as a spiral or star. When all is done light night-lights in jam jars around your shrine and thank the Earth for her abundance.

MASKS AND HEADDRESSES

PUTTING ON A MASK or an elaborate headdress can transform the wearer into another person, another being, or to another level. They can provide an opportunity for the wearer to enter another world that can be liberating and deeply moving, sometimes even frightening. They can help a person enter into the spirit of a part of themselves that they wish to explore. They can also simply be great fun and add an extra dimension to a celebration. They are a way of connecting to the moment, capturing everyone's imagination in ways previously unexplored. Afterwards, when your masks or headdresses are hanging on the wall, they are a great memory of that celebratory moment, and are waiting for the next occasion to come to life.

Through the choice of mask you wish to wear, much can be learnt about yourself and your need to express that particular part of yourself. You might wish to take on the role of a particular archetype in a shamanic sense, to share and connect to an energy, such as a Moon mask, or an animal mask or a mythical being. This may release a whole range of qualities in the wearer that may go beyond the actual time spent wearing the mask.

When you put your mask on at the beginning, the moment should never be rushed. Feel the presence of what you are now a part of. This needs your full attention. Masks and headdresses invite an exploration of imaginative ways to move, taking on a particular rhythm or pulse. This may be enhanced through dance. Uttering sounds will also help you to feel the spirit of what you are becoming. Once you have become engaged with yourself, you can then begin to interact with others within the context of ritual, ceremony, plays or narrative story.

We have a wealth of myths, legends and stories that have been handed down to us from our multi-cultural heritage. Many old teachings are to be found within them and they represent the most accessible way we have of touching our native wisdom. Learn to tell them and then retell them. Each time new things will be revealed. Masks may be used as an aid to storytelling through the medium of narrative plays. Performances can include dance and music. Processions take on new energy and excitement when everyone is masked or in elaborate headdresses.

If you are using masks to conjure up an atmosphere, remember to make the most use of silence and the power of the mask's presence. Make the most use of lighting if it is dark. Candlelight always adds atmosphere. Use candle lanterns if you are outside, or small table lamps that can be switched off or on, if you are inside. Torches can be elaborated by adding coloured tissue paper cones, and these too can be switched on and off when needed. Candlelit processions are always a wonderful sight, and very powerful.

Masks or headdresses may be worn to invoke the Five Elements. If a big mask is made, it will need someone to carry it, and perhaps someone to speak for it, as sound can become muffled from behind a mask. Headdresses work well here as they leave the face free. Face paint can be used on the face for added effect.

One other point is to be aware that perhaps your mask may frighten or un-nerve other people, especially younger children, and this needs to be sensitively dealt with. If you are aware that your mask may appear to be a bit frightening, then establish with the children who it is underneath the mask, and please don't be tempted to feed that fear by acting fiercely or chasing them. Masks have very powerful energy both for the wearer and the observer. They should always be worn with a sense of ceremony, and an awareness of the deeper energy behind them.

Making Masks

There is a deeply absorbing connection made as you create your own mask or headdress. Ways to make them are too numerous to describe here, but if you want to make a mask, here are some clues and starting points:

One of the quickest and easiest ways to create a mask is to go to a fancy dress shop, buy a cheap moulded plastic mask, and then go to an art shop and buy some PVA glue and some coloured tissue paper sheets. Tear the tissue up into small pieces and with slightly watered-down PVA, paste them all over the plastic mask, overlapping them several times and building up the colour variations. Cover the whole thing with a layer of glue and leave to dry overnight. If you want to elaborate the shape of the plastic mask, use glue-soaked tissue paper or attach cardboard shapes first using masking tape. Pipe cleaners are also useful for added extras and, once twisted into shape, can be covered in the glued tissue paper. If you want to paint your mask or build the surface and shape up a bit, use torn newspaper strips instead of coloured tissue paper. Give it a coat of white emulsion paint when it's dry. You then have a really good surface to paint on your design. Acrylics are the best paints to use, eliminating the need for varnish.

If you want to make a mask for yourself that will fit your face exactly, the following method is the most successful I have found. You will need to buy a roll of old fashioned brown paper parcel tape, the kind that needs to be wet to become sticky. This can be bought in various sizes from art shops and some stationery shops. Cut the tape into lots of strips, approximately 1-2cms x 3-4cms, then you will need someone to help you. Lie on your back with your head on a towel. Place a thin plastic sandwich bag or piece of tinfoil over the upper part of your face, up to the tip of your nose. Be very careful not to cover the nostrils so that breathing is not impaired. Then, with a bowl of water and the piles of cut strips, ask your helper to wet the strips of parcel tape quickly, and lay them over the plastic on your upper face, moulding into the shape of the forehead, cheeks, round the edge of the hairline, down the nose, keeping holes around the eyes.

Try not to get it too wet. By building up the layers, the mask will take shape quite quickly and will dry and keep its shape in 5-10 minutes.

Take it off the face, peel off the plastic, and there you have a perfectly moulded impression of your upper face. This mask is light and comfortable, leaving your mouth free for talking and eating. (The lower face can be face-painted for added effect.) Once dry, go over the edges with masking tape to make them strong. Additions such as beaks, horns, ears etc. can be added using cardboard and masking tape and then finish with a layer of torn paper strips, and leave to dry out completely.

Finish off with a coat of white emulsion before painting with acrylics or covering with coloured tissue paper. Final embellishments with gold or silver paint always look great in candlelight. When the mask is dry, make holes in the side and attach elastic.

Making Headdresses

Headdresses can be made using an existing hat as a base, and then adding things. Pipe cleaners, wire, tissue paper, cardboard, can all be used as well as natural materials, greenery and dried flowers.

Another technique is to sew things on to a sturdy material headband that is elasticated at the back. Add felt shapes, ribbons, or other natural materials. Pipe cleaners can be twisted this way and that and will add height to the headdress. Very large sparkly pipe cleaners can be bought and used very effectively. A good haberdasher has all kinds of wonderful paraphernalia that can be creatively used to great effect. Finally, if you want to make a headdress out of greenery, begin by twisting some long thin whips of willow over and over each other to make a circle which is just a little bit loose on your head. This provides the base for other greenery to be attached to it and wrapped around it. Once you have got your main shape, extras can be poked in the gaps and tied in using green garden wire.

Making a Headress

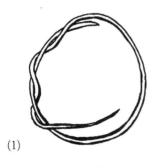

(1)

1. Choose a long whip of willow to begin your circle. If you use fresh willow, be aware that it will shrink as it dries out and the whole thing will become looser and bigger. If you are using basket maker's willow, the variety that has the bark removed needs to be soaked in the bath or a stream for about three hours before you use it. The variety that has the bark on, needs to be soaked for 24 hours before use.

(2)

2. Use only the thinnest whips. Attach with the thick end by poking it in the circle and weave with the thin end of each whip. It is better not to end and begin in the same place on your circle, so vary the length of the willow whips that you use. A pair of secateurs is essential for this activity. Trim loose ends.

3. Gathering and using fresh willow, honeysuckle, clematis, ivy and other long thin natural materials creates a more natural looking and comfortable headdress.

(3)

DANCE

DANCING IS PART OF ALL OF US and is a direct link to our inner levels and emotions. Dance is an opportunity to connect and express yourself, to let yourself go and through it we can link in with the Earth's energy and feel the pulse of her rhythms resonate at the core of our deepest selves. There are many ways it may be used as part of a celebration or ceremony.

If you are celebrating on your own, you might want to put some music on which helps connect to your mood and the festival, or you may find that a chant you are singing becomes the starting point for movement and rhythm. Explore this connection between the sounds you make and the different ways in which your body can express itself. Feel your power and abandon yourself to the dance.

Dance can be used at the beginning of a celebration as a way of bringing people together. Here the group could be led into a spiral and out again, or into a weaving pattern to connect and create a web of energy and intent. Other patterns of flow could be explored. Use the power of movement to raise the energy and connect the group to each other.

A simple drumbeat is all that is needed to begin movement. Dancers may have bells or shakers or sticks by which they can add rhythms while dancing. If someone can play a whistle, this simple instrument can cut through all other percussion. Clapping and vocalising sound all add to the build-up of energy created by improvised dancing.

Circle dance and folk dance are more formal, but also bring the group together. Someone will need to teach the steps and provide the appropriate music. Keep the dances simple and, once the dance is learnt, the movement and energy changes from one of concentration to one of 'flow', a pulse of rhythm through which the whole group is connected, and the mind can slip into a meditative state. Here lies the ancient source of its power. These dances have been handed down to us from the past and perhaps had a deeper meaning and purpose that we can try to understand.

Invent new dances with new stories to tell. Explore each of the Five Elements in turn, express yourself, become one with them. Dance yourself as Sun or Moon, an animal, or an archetype.

Take off your shoes and dance on the Earth. It is always an invigorating and connecting experience.

BETWEEN THE WORLDS

THE CELTS BELIEVED IN three parallel universes that co-exist with this, our own three-dimensional world, which is governed by time.

The Celtic Otherworld, Annwn, is a place of rebirth, inspiration and life renewal. It can symbolically be thought of as a place above this one, but it lives within us, within our powerful imaginations. It can be seen as a place outside of time, a place of deities, archetypes, angels, spirit guides, animal guides, guardians, and the ancestors.

The Otherworld can be entered from this world, accessed through dreams, trance, and meditation, altered states of mind. Folk tales speak of access through hidden doorways in the land found by springs, caves and other natural places. The sacred groves, stone circles, barrows and burial mounds of the past may also have been built on sites that access and amplify this energy. There are potent times in the Earth's cycle when the veil between the worlds is thin. We can find these routes in to this Otherworld and strengthen them by use and acknowledgement of their existence.

The Celtic Underworld is the hidden doorway into other possible inter-dimensional realities, such as the faerie realms. Folk stories tell us that time runs differently here and not to eat any food lest we become trapped. It is populated by a race apart, beyond our normal sight, beyond our control, but co-existing with us and ever-present, if we take the time to make contact. Their presence can be felt in the wild places of moor and mountain or by forgotten springs, where they have retreated from humankind. But they are just as likely to be found by hearth and home, in the garden, perhaps willing to communicate with us again if we respect their existence.

Finding places of power in your locality will greatly enrich your life, especially if you work with the Earth energies there, trusting your intuition to guide your actions. It could be that our participation with the Earth's life force increases the energy and health of these power places so long neglected. Dowse any area you feel is important, mark with a stone, bury crystals, and release the energy. The nearest living parallel from which we may learn about this is through the Aborigines in Australia. They speak of 'dream-time' and the 'spirit-tracks' that connect the power centres of their land. These power centres they call 'places of increase', places where visions can be dreamed into reality.

There are many places we can go to make this kind of connection. Standing stones, stone circles, dolmens, burial mounds, barrows, tumuli, sacred wells and any sacred place of the ancients. We can also sometimes come across it unexpectedly in a wood, by a spring, in the high places. There is no mistaking the feeling as you find yourself slipping out of time and normal reality. In those special places where the veil between the worlds is thin, we can slip from an everyday state of mind into something dreamy and altered in some way. Vision hazes and a faraway look comes into the eyes.

Here is the interface between the worlds. Here we can feel the timeless presence of past and future, receive visions and insights, travel out of time and place.

Dragon Paths and Leylines

Geomancy is the art of tuning into or dowsing the vibration of underground currents of Earth energy. This may be underground water currents, veins of minerals and streams of electromagnetic energy. These energy paths were known in the past as the dragon paths or the serpent force and more recently as leylines. Burial mounds were called dragon hills and the dragon was their legendary guardian. They may have been built on Earth faults where the underground radiation from the Earth may cause altered states of consciousness and aid inner journeying and healing. The slaying of the dragon may have been an ancient system of geomancy where the dragon paths were staked to release these energies in a similar way to acupuncture, as a means of keeping the Earth healthy. By the same token, modern dowsers have noticed that people living directly on underground currents, known as 'black water', will become ill, and they can redirect these harmful energies by staking the ground with copper pipes.

Using an Ordnance Survey map, connect up the ancient sites, springs, wells, tumuli, burial mounds, churches (especially where they are dedicated to St Michael, the dragon-slayer). This reveals the hidden 'straight tracks' or leylines; the hidden energy paths that criss-cross our land. Then take your map out and walk the land. Intuit where they might be, or use dowsing rods or pendulum to dowse them. Also dowse the twists and turns of the serpent paths. Where both the leylines and the serpent paths meet and cross, the 'places of increase' are revealed. These are the power places where Earth energy is potent and concentrated. Much has been lost, but with a new awareness and intuitive insight, some of it is now being re-found. It is up to us to find and strengthen these ancient connections, and to work with the Earth energy in new intuitive ways.

Stone Circles

Megaliths, dolmens and stone circles, dating from 5000-500 BC, are to be found all over Western Europe, the British Isles, Scandinavia and the Near East. These are fantastic feats of engineering and skill. Many of them were built as huge cosmic calendars, measuring the great planetary cycles as well as those of the Sun and Moon. The stone circles continue to draw us. We go there seeking some kind of communion with the Earth, Earth energies and our ancestors. We walk about them, perhaps following hidden pathways of energy and feel drawn towards sitting in certain spots, or towards certain stones. Their energy is dreamy and we can lie down on the earth or put our backs against the stones and find stillness. They are places to do ritual, to invoke and speak out our deepest wishes and intentions, to align ourselves with the potent life force of the land, to give thanks for this moment and to strengthen our inner reserves so that we leave full and restored, able make the changes we wish for.

Many stone circles emit a change in frequency at the Solstices and the Equinoxes. (See *Circles of Silence*. Recommended Reading page 234.)

Burial Mounds, Dolmens and Barrows (Tumuli)

These are large man-made mounds from the Neolithic and Bronze Age, dating from 4000 to 700 BC. They consist of a stone box chamber that was covered with earth. They sometimes have elaborate entrances that may or may not have a blocking stone across it. They are Earth wombs for the bones or cremated remains of souls awaiting rebirth, or for holding the power objects of the tribe. In the light of recent understanding many have been built on Earth faults where the underground radiation from the Earth causes altered states of consciousness, so they may have also been used as places to communicate with the dead, as well as for inner journeying, rituals, ceremonies and healing. They were called dragon hills and were said to be guarded by dragons. In Ireland they were called hollow hills and were said to be entrances to the faerie realms.

As many of these sites emit an increase in natural radioactivity (is this the same as the 'places of increase' of the Aborigines?), they are places to gain inspiration and insights, to slip out of time, to meditate and to go within. Acoustically, they may be used for interesting ventures into sound, resonant healing and chanting. They are places to go to make contact with the Earth, for inner journeys, for healing both the Earth and ourselves, and working with the energies present in creative and intuitive ways.

The Spiral

The spiral is one of our oldest symbols, representing eternal life, unfolding growth within and without, Spirit and Matter, death and rebirth, continuous creation. At the centre is the point of complete balance, a stillness within, around which all things revolve. In Celtic art it is found as the single, double and triple spiral and can be used as a symbol in decoration wherever its intrinsic properties need to be recognised and invoked.

The ebb and flow of its energy pattern make it a perfect tool for walking meditation, making your way to the centre to meet your own still point within, before coming back out again having gained insights from within. A spiral path can be made permanently on the land using stones, turf, living willow or planted herbs such as rosemary, lavender or box. Living plant spirals need to be kept trimmed frequently to encourage a tight growth of small leaves. A spiral can also be temporarily marked out on the land using cut grasses or plants, sticks and stones. Indoors it can be marked out using salt (never use this outside, as it will kill vegetation), compost, or sand. Decorate with flowers, crystals and night-lights. A triple spiral offers the opportunity to spiral in and out with three intentions or three aspects of one focus.

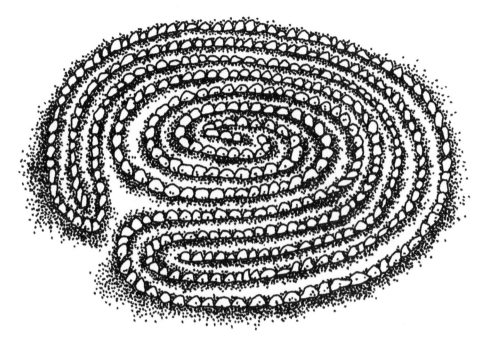

The Labyrinth

A labyrinth is a continuous path which, when followed, leads a person into the centre and out again. Unlike a maze, there are no false turns or dead ends or choices. The same as the spiral, a labyrinth has a still point at the centre, which can be used for meditation or ritual. Walk the labyrinth slowly with bare feet as a walking meditation. It is said that spirits travel in straight lines, and the labyrinths may have been used as a device to shake off unwanted spirits. They can also be seen as a device to enhance the flow of left brain/right brain activity, releasing blocked thoughts and enhancing creative inspiration. See pages 134-137 for Making a Labyrinth.

THE WHEEL OF THE YEAR
WITH RELATED NATIVE TREES AND HERBS

SPENDING TIME WITH OUR NATIVE TREES and healing plants at each festival helps
to bring a deeper connection to the world around us. The following chart shows the
traditional seasonal connections of many of our native trees and common plants.

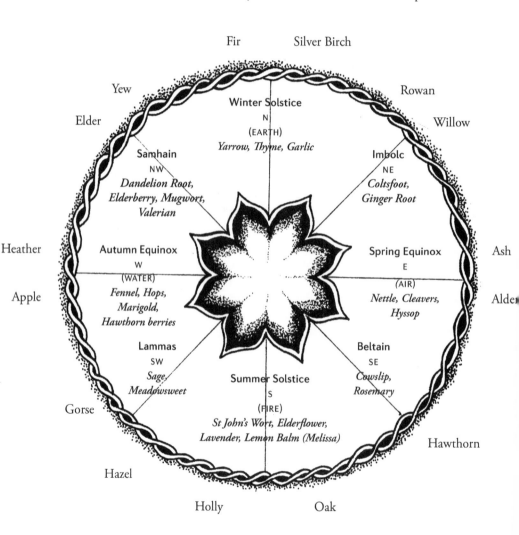

Fir   Silver Birch

Yew   Rowan

Elder   Willow

Winter Solstice
N
(EARTH)
Yarrow, Thyme, Garlic

Samhain
NW
Dandelion Root,
Elderberry, Mugwort,
Valerian

Imbolc
NE
Coltsfoot,
Ginger Root

Heather   Ash

Autumn Equinox
W
(WATER)
Fennel, Hops,
Marigold,
Hawthorn berries

Spring Equinox
E
(AIR)
Nettle, Cleavers,
Hyssop

Apple   Alder

Lammas
SW
Sage,
Meadowsweet

Beltain
SE
Cowslip,
Rosemary

Summer Solstice
S
(FIRE)
St John's Wort, Elderflower,
Lavender, Lemon Balm (Melissa)

Gorse   Hawthorn

Hazel

Holly   Oak

THE TREE OGHAM

INCLUDED IN EACH FESTIVAL are native trees and shrubs from the Celtic Tree Ogham, an ancient Druidic system of tree lore. These symbols have survived carved into rocks along the west coast of Scotland. It is thought that they were used as a form of written communication. Each symbol is linked to a tree or shrub and holds a wealth of deeper meaning, similar to an astrological or planetary symbol. Gather a small piece of wood from each tree and mark them with their symbol. These can be used for guidance as with the Runes. See page 230 for method.

10		APPLE Q - Quert	20	YEW I - Idadh
9		HAZEL C - Coll	19	ASPEN E - Eadadh
8		HOLLY T - Tinne	18	HEATHER U - Ur
7		OAK D - Duir	17	GORSE O - Onn
6		HAWTHORN H - Huath	16	FIR A - Ailm
5		ASH N - Nion	15	ELDER R - Ruis
4		WILLOW S - Saille	14	BLACKTHORN ST/z - Straiph
3		ALDER F - Fearn	13	BROOM nG - nGetal
2		ROWAN L - Luis	12	IVY G - Gort
1		BIRCH B - Beithe	11	VINE M - Muin

THE EIGHT CELTIC FESTIVALS

The following section charts the progression of the year's solar cycle and the eight festivals that have been used since Celtic times to honour and celebrate the changes of energy that this brings to the Earth and ourselves.

Each festival looks at the way this energy was used and interpreted in the past, as handed down to us from Pagan and Druid tradition, and folk customs which have survived the passage of time.

Each festival looks at the underlying energy of the Earth, how this energy affects us, and how we can use this in new ways that are relevant to us today.

Preparations for each festival include ideas for things to do before the festival to bring a deeper connection to these developing energies. Choose to do what you are most drawn towards, and find your own ways to make these connections.

Finally each festival includes suggestions for celebration and ceremony. You will find many more ways of your own. These celebrations lend themselves to gathering with kindred spirits, sharing and expressing yourself and your feelings, but to celebrate them on your own is also an empowering experience as you listen to the guidance of your inner wisdom. It's good to do both. However you celebrate them, the important thing is to mark the occasion in some way, touch the sacred, your own sense of the spiritual, as you follow the path of your heart and respect for the Earth.

WINTER SOLSTICE

WINTER QUARTER POINT
20th-23rd December

SUN ENTERS CAPRICORN ♑

The shortest day and longest night

*Midwinter * Yule*

Festival of Rebirth

Celebration of the Return of the Sun

WINTER SOLSTICE

The Sun enters the sign of Capricorn ♑ as her rays shine directly at their southern extreme for the year. This is the shortest day and the longest night of the Northern Hemisphere. In the Southern Hemisphere they celebrate the Summer Solstice at this time.

THE GREAT COSMIC WHEEL of the year, the fiery hub of the universe, the symbolic Wheel of Time, is acknowledged here. Jul or Yule means wheel in Norwegian. Northern Europeans of our Celtic past believed this mystic wheel stopped turning briefly at this crucial point as one cycle ended and a new cycle of the Sun began. It was taboo to rotate any wheels at the Winter Solstice, from cartwheels to butter churns, as they waited for the return of the Sun. The Solstice was a moment to stop, to look backwards in inner reflection and to look forwards to a new active season as the Sun's returning power brings increased daylight, growth and activity. From now on the days will lengthen and the warmth will come again. This was an important moment in our Celtic past. Megalithic monuments acknowledged this return of the Sun. The outer Sarsen ring of Stonehenge is orientated to the Midwinter Solstice sunset. Newgrange in Ireland is aligned to sunrise on the Winter Solstice when a shaft of light pierces a long tunnel deep into this burial mound to illuminate an inner chamber. It is possible still to be one of a handful of people who experience this moment standing deep inside this earth-womb chamber.

To understand this moment, it is important to realise that this festival is not the beginning, in a linear way of looking at things, but a rebirth within a cycle in which the starting point chosen here is part of a vibrant whole. Therefore it is necessary to make a connection to what has gone before. Since the last festival at Samhain, the Earth has been withdrawn within itself. The darkness of the receding daylight hours has been felt by all of nature and humankind. Root energy has been strengthened, the dream world explored, mysteries understood. The deep wisdom of the unconscious has brought spiritual insights. The old year has died and, through reflection and assimilation, the way is now prepared for rebirth of the active principle. The 'Cauldron of Regeneration', as this process was known, was central to Celtic and Pagan understanding. Something old must die in order for something new to be reborn. This period of rest and darkness is a vital link in the cycle of life.

Homes were decorated with evergreens such as holly, ivy, mistletoe, yew, and pine, all of which represented the cycle of everlasting life. The church tried to stop these old customs but they have endured. Other traditional customs for the Winter Solstice included Yule logs, door wreaths to symbolize the Wheel of the Year, feasting, gifts, dancing, masks, mystery plays, mummers' plays, processions, decorated trees, and candlelight. These were to honour the return of the Sun and the cycle of life.

A traditional story told at Winter Solstice tells of a Sun king who ripened the harvest at Lammas and was sacrificed back into the land within the seed. (This signifies the sacrifice of the active principle as the Sun loses its power and the energy turns within.) He stays underground as the Dark Lord of the Underworld, Pluto, Hades, the Grim Reaper, Lord of Death. At the Winter Solstice he is reborn as the Lord of Light, the Sun king, the Sun god.

The Christian church adopted this time to celebrate the birth of the 'Son of God', Jesus, the new-born king, on the 25th of December, just a few days after the Winter Solstice. The Mithraic religion had a similar saviour, Mithra, who was also born at the Winter Solstice after his death and conception nine months earlier on the 25th of March (Spring Equinox/Easter). He too was called the Light of the World. Norsemen celebrated the birthday of their Lord Frey at the Winter Solstice. A similar story is the one of Heracles, a Greek saviour, also born from a virgin. His twelve labours symbolized the passage of the Sun during the year through the twelve signs of the zodiac. After this journey, he was clothed in scarlet robes, killed, resurrected as his own Divine Father, to marry the Virgin Mother Goddess and be reborn all over again at the Winter Solstice. The ancient myths and legends have many stories and versions of wheel kings who were wrapped in fiery cloaks or fiery wheels. Divine Fathers and Divine Sons were one and the same person, cyclically alternating and uniting through marriage with the Virgin Mother Goddess to be reborn as new again.

In the western Pagan tradition, the Sun is masculine, active, outward, creative energy, but there are older traditions that celebrated the Winter Solstice as rebirth of a Sun goddess. Anastasia was one of Rome's great goddesses. Her holy day was that of the Sun's rebirth at the Winter Solstice. This festival began with its eve called *'matrum noctem'*, the night of the mother. There were many earlier goddesses, all systematically destroyed, turned into devils or demons, masculinised or turned into saints to be incorporated into the church. Another interpretation of this part of the year is explained through the story of Demeter and Persephone who was abducted by Pluto and taken into his Underworld for the winter months. But Persephone was queen of the Underworld long before there was a Pluto, and Pluto was an earlier female deity, a daughter of the Cretan Earth mother Rhea. Pluto became masculine in Christian times and given the qualities of the devil. Other female goddesses include Epona, Macha, Artemis, Astarte, Blodeuwedd, Kali, Demeter, Diana, Branwen, Creiddylad, Cerridwen, Morrigan, Ceres, Grain, Brighidh, Kore – to name but a few.

Celtic understanding saw the Earth as a manifestation of a Triple Goddess. This included the Virgin Goddess of the spring, the Mother Goddess of the summer and harvest, and the Crone who represented wisdom and the inner world of the winter months. This triple deity is found all over the world and is understood as three aspects of the same energy. During the Christian era, the Crone became the dark witch-woman, the object of fear and superstition. Her connection to the inner world of wisdom, intuition and insights from within, almost became lost to humankind. As the Sun is reborn at the Winter Solstice, she becomes her virgin self again, echoing the virgin birth of the Sun king. It is interesting that at the time of the Winter Solstice, the constellation of the virgin rises in the East.

But times are changing and an even bigger cosmic wheel is turning as 2000 years of the Piscean Age give way to a new 2000 years of the Aquarian Age. Now at Winter Solstice let us acknowledge not a Sun god or a Sun goddess, but celebrate the return of the Sun's energy, whether male or female. The growth period to come will bring the return of our active selves. Let us celebrate a time of a united humanity to come, a healing of the wounds of separation, fear and dominance as a new cycle begins.

THE UNDERLYING ENERGY
OF WINTER SOLSTICE

THE EARTH HAS BEEN withdrawn inside herself. Winter brings the
hardships of cold and shortness of daylight. Very little outer growth has
happened, but deep within the Earth, roots have been growing, bringing
stability and nutrients to the plants and trees. Now we can see the new
buds forming on the trees and bushes and bulbs are beginning to
send up their first hardy shoots. All of nature has slowed down,
waiting for the energy to change and for warmth to return. Due
to the restraints of winter, we too have slowed down and have
been conserving energy. We have spent time withdrawn within
ourselves.

The time between Samhain and Yule is the darkest time of the
year. As the outer world is darkened by shorter days and cloudy
cold weather, the inner realms can expand. This has been a great
opportunity for us to experience the world within our selves.
It has been a time to assimilate our experiences and an
incubation period for our own personal seeds, plans and ideas.
Now with the return of the active outward energy that the Sun
brings, all of these can slowly begin to manifest.

Winter Solstice is a celebration of the rebirth of the Sun's active
cycle. Being part of this cycle means that we too are reborn at this
time. We bring the wisdom of our inner journeys out into the world,
to grow with the increasing light from the Sun. It is a time for
birthing our visions and naming the dreams that we have been
incubating so that we can assist their manifestation consciously
in our lives. This is the time to celebrate the active principle
whose positive qualities of logical thinking, determination and
assertiveness bring independence and purpose to our lives.

Standing in the circle
Beneath the web of light
Dancing in the moonlight
On a cold new year's night
And it seemed we were lifted
Flown across the years
Power-circle shifted
By power-circle seers

And the Goddess and John Barleycorn
Will put flesh upon the bones
Fly ribbons round the barrows
Plant footprints round the stones
The Goddess and John Barleycorn
Will keep the spirit strong
For those who remember
For those who sing the song

So stand in the circle
Weave the web of light
Dance in the moonlight
Bring fire to the night
Release the past that made us
Release the fire within
Revel in the mystery
And embrace your sacred kin.

Brian Boothby
Tomorrows Ancestor

PREPARATIONS FOR
WINTER SOLSTICE

*Evergreens * Wreaths * Solstice Bush*
*Bower * Candles * Yule Log*
Power Animals
*Trees: Silver Birch * Fir*
*Herbs: Yarrow * Thyme * Garlic*

Traditionally the Winter Solstice is a time to gather with family, friends and kin. Few of us have the space for bringing lots of people together, so hire a village hall or similar space for the day, sharing the cost amongst everyone. This provides practical facilities and a space large enough for dancing and feasting. Decorating a big space will need some planning but much can be done with evergreens, coloured hangings and side lighting (table lamps or candle lanterns), with everyone pooling their resources.

Evergreens

Evergreens are brought into the home at this time to represent everlasting life. They are hung around the doorways and the windows and in the past each area of the country had traditional customs, inclusions and superstitions. Each of the different evergreens has a deeper symbolism and inherent energy that can be consciously worked with as you make your Winter Solstice decorations. Take time to make contact with the tree or plant you wish to use. Greet it, appreciate it and ask for some of its twigs for your Solstice decorations. You will know in your heart if it is all right to cut. It usually is, but sometimes it isn't. Respect that. Thank the tree or plant afterwards. It creates a loving energy-field which is beneficial to both the plant and yourself.

HOLLY Holly is sacred to Mother Holle or Hel, the Underworld Goddess. Holly is one of the native trees favoured by the Druids, and part of the Celtic Tree Ogham. The holly symbolizes everlasting life, recovery, goodwill and potent life energy. It unites past actions with present actions and restores direction in your life, helping your heart to be open to unconditional love. Red holly berries of Pagan Solstice decorations represent the red female blood of life, while the white mistletoe berries represent the white semen drops of the life-giving male. Holly and mistletoe are displayed alongside each other to represent the sacred marriage that brings forth new life.

N.B. Holly berries are mildly poisonous; keep away from young children.

MISTLETOE At midwinter the Druids ceremoniously lopped the mistletoe from the oak tree, caught it in a cloth so that it did not touch the earth, and laid it on the Solstice altar to represent fertility (hence kissing beneath it).

N.B. Mistletoe berries are poisonous; keep away from young children.

IVY Ivy is another plant commonly used for Solstice decorations and represents the search for the self through the freedom to follow your own path. Ivy is about finding your own inner resources and acting upon them. It holds trees as they are dying. All evergreens link to the concept of everlasting life, so central to Celtic spiritual understanding.

N.B. Ivy berries are poisonous; keep them away from young children.

YEW Yew is a sacred and ancient tree, long-lived and revered for its connection to the Otherworld and the ancestors. It signifies regeneration and rebirth. See Samhain page 224.

N.B. If you have children or animals, it would be best not to bring in sprigs of yew as the fallen leaves, bark and the seed within the fruit are all poisonous.

Bower

In the garden, at a stone circle or out on the land, create a bower of evergreens using a hazel arch as a base. (See page 26.) Make a shrine and light candles here for the returning Sun. Create a permanent Winter Solstice bower by planting evergreens around the hazel arch, and weaving them around each other. Use garden wire to tie them into place while they grow. Remember to remove it later.

Wreaths

As we celebrate the Wheel of the Year turning once again towards the Sun, there is an old tradition of making a wreath of evergreens. It may be hung on the door, or laid horizontally with places for candles to be lit. Begin with some long thin whips of willow (at least 4ft lengths if possible), wrapping them into a circle (1). Always use the thin end for the weaving. Continue by anchoring the thick end of a new piece of willow on the circle you have made and, using the thin end to weave, wrap it over and over, round and round several times until a thick base has been made (2). Weave the evergreens around this base (3) using it to anchor in the ends. Green garden wire is useful for tying in loose ends, creating hooks, fixing in candleholders etc.

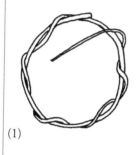  

(1)   (2)   (3)

Solstice Bush

Having rejected the idea of bringing a cut tree into the house for decorating, our family has had much enjoyment on Solstice morning, going out to gather greenery to make a Solstice bush. You will need a few sturdy branches (preferably evergreen) to give it form, anchoring them into a large pot of wet soil with rocks around the base. All other greenery can be poked into the wet soil to bring a richness and variety of different twigs, dried flowers, fruits and berries. Small natural decorations and wrapped sweets can be hung from it.

Yule Log

This is traditionally a log of oak, a sacred tree with connections to the Sun king. It is a very slow burning wood that gives out great heat. Traditionally it was placed on the fire with much ceremony, and the ashes were kept for fertility rituals. You can use the log to absorb and clear energies, thoughts and feelings you wish to purify, transform and release into the fire. Releasing old stuck energy opens the way for new beginnings.

Candles

Lighting candles for the return of the Sun is an old tradition at this time. Buy plenty of them so that you can light your space with their living light. Buy a special one for special wishes and hopes.

Make some candles of your own. Dipped candles are the easiest and most satisfying to do, especially with children. You will need coloured wax, candlewick, an empty food tin can, an old saucepan and plenty of newspaper on the table. Break the wax into the tin and stand in gently boiling water until the wax is all melted. Take the tin out of the water and stand it on the newspaper. Do not let the children boil the water themselves and warn them to be extremely careful with the tin of hot wax. Using a length of wick each, dip the wick in the wax, pull it out to dry, dip it in again, pull it out, and so on. Gradually the wax builds up layer upon layer to make a candle. The wax needs to be melted to about a depth of 7cm in the tin. After a while the wax begins to cool and is used up on the candles, so the wax in the tin gets very low. Return the tin to the pan of boiling water, add more wax and re-melt. Do this as often as needed.

Creating enough light for an evening celebration in the dark of winter is another consideration. Plenty of table lamps and subdued lighting add atmosphere, but nothing beats large amounts of candles burning. Candle lanterns are excellent and very safe. Night-lights in jam jars are also very safe, but you need a lot of them to create a good light. Paint the jam jars with glass paint (another activity which everyone loves to do), and use green garden wire to wind around the top of the jar for making long carrying-handles for processions.

Hand-guards can be made for household candles if they are to be carried in procession or as part of a ritual dance using any stiff card.

1. Cut out a circle of 15cm diameter, and in the centre, slice a star-shape with a sharp knife.

2. The candle can then be poked through here.

Please be extremely careful when using a naked flame.

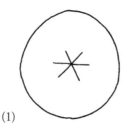

(1)

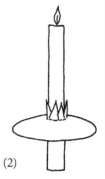

(2)

POWER ANIMALS

IN CELTIC UNDERSTANDING, each animal, insect or bird holds significance and meaning. If it comes into your dreams and visions, it comes for a reason. If an animal crosses your path or a bird flies overhead at significant moments, again, there are insights to be gained from this. Pictures of power animals and carved talismans can be given as gifts and used in ceremonies.

The Bear
Bears were revered and honoured for their strength and great reserves of power. Celtic warriors going into battle may have invoked the strength and wisdom of the bear. Votive statues of bears and ritual jewellery have been found throughout the Celtic lands. Bears' teeth were prized as talismans. Bears' pelts were prized as clothing and for sleeping on. The bear goes into its cave in the winter, teaching us to go within, in order to digest our experiences, and to become a spiritual warrior by integrating intuition and inner wisdom with strength and purpose.

The Wolf
Here intelligence is linked with instinct. The wolf is free to explore alone or be with the rest of the pack for companionship, strength of numbers and nurturing. When exploring hidden paths alone, we may discover new truths to share with the rest of our family and kin. Wolf brings strength and courage to be who you are, to face the cycles of death and rebirth and to learn from them.

The Eagle
From earliest times there has been a link between birds and ancestral spirits. Eagles were said to bring messages from the gods to foretell the future. They were known as symbols of death and rebirth, associated with Sun gods, Fire and lightning. The eagle was thought to be a passing spirit, the soul of a god returning to heaven after an earthly incarnation as a king. It is linked to solar mysteries and initiation rites. The eagle was often associated with the firebird or phoenix, representing a shamanic 'Baptism by Fire' that could bring transformation and rebirth from the ashes of the old. Shamans were said to be able to transform themselves into eagles to gain an overview.

Winter Solstice is traditionally a time for mystery plays and carnival.
The Midwinter carnival of medieval times included the story of Saturnalia as King Carnival who was killed with the old year before the new Sun rose again. Consider performing a piece of drama, dance or masked play that helps to illuminate the message of the Winter Solstice. Look for old folk legends with richness of symbolism and imagery. Make the most use of colour, light and masks, exploring ways to go beyond words to conjure atmosphere and deep connections.

Clear the way for changes and new beginnings. Cleanse your self and your friends and family by burning dried sage in a small pottery dish and 'bathing' in the smoke. Visualise a spiral of rainbow light around you and visualise your aura bright and sparkling. Clean your room(s). Cleanse everything by washing it all in salt water. Give away as presents what you no longer need and is cluttering up your space. Create a sacred shrine area where you can light a candle, and keep a few things there that will help keep your spiritual focus.

Cleanse all your crystals by washing them in running water and putting them outside for a while. Let them bathe in the winter Sun, the moonlight, the rain, the frosts and the snow. Let them regenerate through the power of the elements. Any crystals that have been used a lot for healing and psychic work, bury in salt for twenty-four hours before washing in running water and leaving outside.

Make a large Sun-creation out of basket maker's willow or cane, creating a space inside for a night light in a jam jar. Use masking tape to hold the shape together by taping the joints to make them strong. Cover with yellow tissue paper leaving a hole top and bottom. Stiffen the tissue paper by giving it several light coats of watered-down PVA glue, letting it dry well between the coats. Use it during your celebrations. It can be hung from a stick or string.

Nothing beats watching the Solstice Sun break free of the horizon on the Solstice. Plan how and where you will do this. Being out early on the land will bring its own special gifts, even if the day is cloudy, so plan to go whatever the weather.

TREES OF WINTER SOLSTICE

SILVER BIRCH – *Betula pendula*

The first tree of the Celtic Tree Ogham: BEITH. B. The silver birch is the first tree to colonise new ground, dropping its leaves and twigs to enrich the soil so other trees may follow. It is thus a tree of life-giving properties, vitality and nourishment, signifying a new start, a new beginning, birth, inception, and new opportunities. The Celts used the twigs of the birch for driving out the spirits of the old year and considered the birch to have great powers of purification and renewal. Link with silver birch to prepare yourself for new journeys, spiritual or physical. The birch sheds its bark, teaching us to let go of any unhelpful influences and clear the way for the new to begin. The wood from the silver birch is very good for carving and was traditionally used for babies' cradles.

Fir and Pine trees

SCOTS PINE – *Pinus sylvestris*

The Fir is the sixteenth tree of the Celtic Tree Ogham: AILM. A. Pines were planted in groves as temples to the Great Mother. Roman priests called 'dendropbori' or 'tree bearers' on the eve of Midwinter Solstice, would cut down one of her sacred pines, decorate it and carry it into the temple. Honoured for its ability to help us develop the perceptions, insights and wisdom to see far beyond the present, it brings strength and healing learnt from past experiences. From this elevated viewpoint, farsighted actions can be undertaken, great things can be done, new objective insights acted upon. Bring a spray of pine into the house as part of your evergreen decorations or Solstice bush. Thank it for its gifts. Afterwards, make a wand, touchwood, or Ogham key from the wood.

HERBS OF WINTER SOLSTICE

YARROW – *Achillea millefolium*

It is one of the best remedies for bringing out a fever, producing copious amounts of sweating and lowering the blood pressure. Drink a wineglassful of the infusion hourly until the fever subsides. Pour one pint of boiling water on a handful of the dried herb. Leave covered for ten minutes. (Especially good combined with elderflower and

peppermint.) It can also be used to speed up the clotting of blood and can be used on all wounds, old and new.

Use the crushed fresh leaves directly or the water from soaked dried leaves for cuts, nosebleeds, earache and toothache. The Druids used yarrow to divine the weather. In China, yarrow stalks are used with the I Ching oracle system. Yarrow will strengthen the etheric body (our spirit body) as a protection against the influence of others.

THYME – *Thymus vulgaris*

A valuable tonic herb for the whole system and an antiseptic. It stimulates white blood cell production to help the body resist infection. Useful for all digestive complaints, inflammation of the liver, nervous indigestion, flatulence, bad breath and hangovers. It will promote perspiration in fevers, lowering the temperature and quickly cleansing the body of infection. Use for dry irritating coughs, sore throats and ear infections. It will relieve insomnia and calm night fears. Thyme brings courage, inner strength and a stronger sense of purpose. Pour boiling water on a handful of dried herb and leave covered for ten minutes. Drink a wineglassful three times a day.

GARLIC – *Allium sativum*

A powerful antiseptic useful for all viral and fungal infections, colds and fevers.

Eat raw for all respiratory problems, circulatory and heart problems, causing blood pressure to be lowered and helping reduce blood cholesterol levels and angina. The juice diluted with water can be used as an antiseptic on wounds and is a good external rub for arthritis and rheumatic pain when used hot. Garlic makes it easier to transcend the physical plane, thus aiding astral travel and even the transition of death.

WINTER SOLSTICE CELEBRATIONS

These are some suggestions for celebrating the Winter Solstice.

The eve of Winter Solstice is a special night to be out for a night walk. Walk in silence and connect to the mystical wild part of yourself which links with the Earth at this, one of the most ancient rites of transformation and rebirth.

Stay up all night, tell stories of power and reconnection to the mystical energies, the magical world, whose vibrant and vital dance is all around you.

If you can't stay up all night, then get up early before dawn. Go to a special high place and watch the Solstice sunrise or the lightening of the sky in the South East. These are magical moments you will always remember. Affirm your new dreams and wishes, and the changes you wish to bring into your life as the new cycle unfolds.

This is the time to celebrate friendships, family and sacred kin. Experience belonging to a tribe. Focus on your spirit of generosity and let your heart open in gratitude for all the good people in your life. By feeling thankful for what you have in the present, you open the channels for your own abundance.

Invite friends to spend Solstice eve and/or Solstice day with you. In the heart of winter, when we can sometimes feel a bit isolated and low, celebrating the Winter Solstice will bring a real heart-warming connection to like-minded friends and our shared love for the Earth.

Find a venue that is large enough to bring your local like-minded community together to celebrate the Winter Solstice in true tribal fashion. A village hall can be hired for the day. Ask everyone to bring greenery and hangings to decorate the space, and special food to share to have a feast. Celebrate the Earth's abundance and the friends and family with whom you can share it. Book a good band for dancing to. Ask everyone to bring a gift, a present – the same number of presents as there are in their family – labelled adult, teen or child. These can be put into adult, teen or child labelled baskets as people arrive. (It's a good idea to have a few extra presents to save any disappointments.) These presents need not necessarily be bought, but something of yours that you no longer need or use. This is the spirit of the 'give-away'. Later, after the feast, the presents can be distributed by the children or put in the centre of the circle so that each can go and choose a present from the basket.

Begin the gathering with an opening ceremony. Put out all the other lights beforehand and light one central candle. Each light a candle from this and make a wish. The candles can be pushed into a large bowl of sand. Hum and chant together. Be careful with naked flames. Keep quiet and focused while holding them.

At the centre of the circle place a beautiful piece of cloth and on it place something to represent each element. Create elemental wall hangings, vessels or masks made of willow and tissue paper, which can be carried in and placed in each of the directions. Ask five people to speak for each element, invoking the qualities they bring to this time for the whole group, or encourage all to speak from the heart as the spirit moves them.

Earth in the North

We give thanks to the Earth for this period of rest and regeneration in the dark. We give thanks for the deep wisdom inside ourselves that has helped guide us. We strengthen our roots and create our stability. We anchor ourselves in our hearts and in our love. As the Sun is reborn, we begin to make ready for a new part of the cycle. We ask that we stay grounded and connected to the Earth. We ask that we grow well with love and care for our Earth-home.

Air in the East

We give thanks for the Air, for each breath that gives us life. We give thanks for inspired thoughts and visions, for the power of new ideas and new beginnings. We give thanks for the power of our voices in song and sound, and for the movement of our thoughts that allows us to explore new levels of understanding. We ask that our communications be direct and clear. We listen to the messages we receive from our inner wisdom and will remember to act upon them.

Fire in the South

We give thanks for Fire, the vital energy source, creative life force, great cleanser and transformer! We thank Fire for the bright gifts of spontaneity, expansion, growth, passion, change and active energy. We give thanks for self-expression and our ability to bringing out into the light what we are learning from our time of rest in the darkness. We welcome the light returning, and with it our renewed vital life force! Fire! We give thanks for our freedom to run wild, to begin again a new cycle.

Water in the West

We give thank for the gifts of Water that brings us life and healing. During the winter darkness we have touched the deep emotions hidden inside ourselves. We give thanks for the flowing of our fertile emotional currents. May we remember to follow our hearts, our love and compassion. May we stay receptive to our intuition and carry it with us into the active cycle.

Spirit at the Centre

Spirit within and without and ever present. We give thanks for this vital connection to this essential part of ourselves that cannot be seen and cannot be named. We reach out and in, connecting to our source and the guidance from within. We give thanks for the still point of power at the centre of our being. Through it we are a part of all life and all existence on this Earth and beyond it.

The words I have written here are intended as clues, and pathways to understanding. When invoking the elements, it is important to speak from the heart and with power, so that you help to make the connection strong for yourself and for all those present. Use the elemental charts on pages 30-34 to help you.

Be still. Experience the stillness of Midwinter. Be aware of where you are physically, mentally and spiritually. Meditate for a while on where you are in your heart and the direction you wish to go when the time for movement comes.

Each light a candle for something you wish for with the return of the new outer growth cycle. Have a bowl of sand in the centre of the circle to plant all the candles in. Let them burn right down. By naming your wish out loud, you create energy. The possibilities you dream will become your reality. Allow the miracle of transformation to inspire you. Aspire to do what you most wish to do.

Bring something out from the dark into the light – something that needs honouring, reclaiming, examining, blessing, or thanking. Share with each other the wisdom and understanding that has been gained.

Make some resolutions to help you as you begin the new cycle. (New Year resolutions grew out of this Winter Solstice custom.) Share your hopes and intentions with each other. Speak them out. Give them power. Feel the strength of your intent.

Dance a spiral dance. Begin by singing a simple two or three line chant together. Hold hands in a circle (if you are leading this, make it clear you must hold the same hands throughout) and then gradually begin to spiral into the centre. When the person leading the spiral reaches the centre, stop and let the spiral catch up with itself and then with everyone close to each other, all begin to tone a single note, 'Om' or 'Awen'. Let the notes and toning flow over and over again, so that the sound becomes a continuous wave of harmony. This can last for five or ten minutes as it swells and fades and swells again. After this wondrous sound bath, take up each other's hands again (the same hand as you came in with). The leader turns back on themselves and leads every one out of the spiral back into a circle again. Look into each other's eyes as you pass each person on the way out.

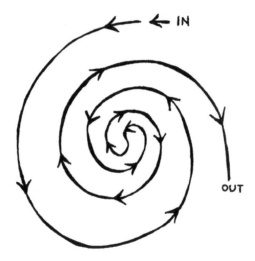

Celebrate the Sun. Switch off all the lights and bring in the Sun you have made, lit up with night-lights inside and hanging from a stick. Let each say whatever comes to them to honour the return of the Sun and its rebirth day. Give thanks for your assertiveness, determination, for our intellectual and rational minds that can create beneficial change for all. The power of intention and self-expression brings independence and purpose to our lives.

Ask everyone to bring drums and percussion. Feel the sense of a tribal gathering as you drum and dance together. Release the old year. Release the restraints of winter. Open your energy to possibilities unlimited and magical as you feel your emergence into the new active phase of the year.

If possible, have a fire and a Yule log of oak. Use the log to focus what needs to be changed and purified by fire. Release old patterns. Leave behind what is no longer helpful to you. Put the log on the fire with ceremony and intent. Let each person call out what Fire will purify and change. Celebrate the release of energy that this brings by drumming and dancing. Let out any sounds, words, chants you need to express. Vocalise the power you feel. Support each other by echoing back the sounds and words people call out. Celebrate moving forwards; free of the restraints that were holding you back.

Tell stories round the fire in an age-old tradition of shared vision and teaching. Tell your own tales or old legends that help us understand the transformative power of the Winter Solstice. Tell of the magical and the mysterious, which can spin us out of time, bringing illumination and insight.

Poems can be read, mystery plays or dance-drama can be performed. Follow the Winter Solstice themes of returning light. Make use of candle lanterns or torches with tissue paper lightly wrapped around the ends to disguise them.

Have a candlelit procession, and if possible, walk out into the night. Enjoy the darkness and the lights of all the candles. Take a circular route to end at where you began. These are magical moments that will be remembered for years to come.

Bless the food and drink everyone has brought to share. Give thanks for your abundance and each other.

Book a good band to play. Party, dance, celebrate, enjoy friends and family around you. Circle dancing brings a gentle reconnecting energy at the end of the evening and brings everyone together before leading into the closing ceremony.

The closing ceremony brings the celebration back full circle and invokes a sense of completeness – a powerful reconnection to take out with you into the world. It renews and acknowledges the sacred as important in our lives. Give thanks to the Five Elements. Let each give thanks for what ever moves them in the moment: for each other, the forces that be, our guardians and spirit guides, renewed connection...
An uplifting chant is always good to end on.

Finally, if you wish, end the celebration with:

> *By the Earth which is her body*
> *By the Air which is her breath*
> *By the Fire which is her bright Spirit*
> *By the living Waters of her womb*
> *The circle is open*
> *And yet unbroken*
> *Merry meet and merry part and merry meet again!*

Blessed Be!

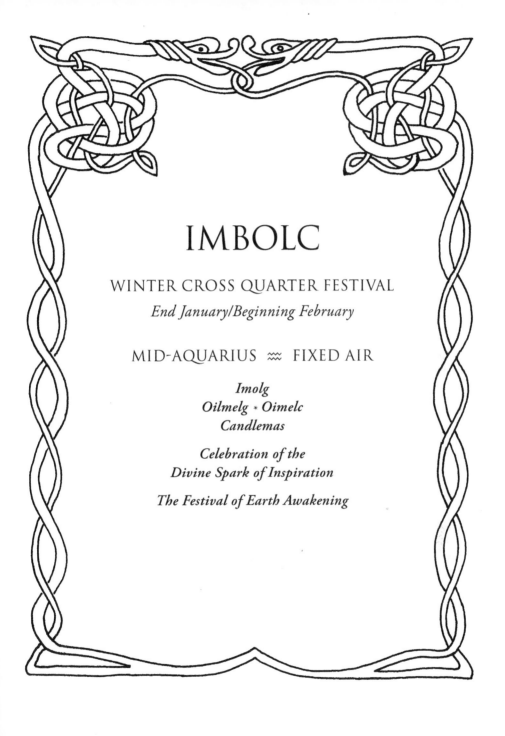

IMBOLC

WINTER CROSS QUARTER FESTIVAL
End January/Beginning February

MID-AQUARIUS ♒ FIXED AIR

*Imolg
Oilmelg * Oimelc
Candlemas*

*Celebration of the
Divine Spark of Inspiration*

The Festival of Earth Awakening

IMBOLC

This festival celebrates the reawakening Earth and the potential of manifestation inherent at this time. The Cross Quarter festivals are an opportunity for us to use the developing energy of a new season. Here it is important that we remember to listen to our intuitive selves, the inner wisdom we have gained during the winter months, as we move into the more active phase of the year. It is this union of the two aspects of ourselves which is the power and magical alchemy of Imbolc, and helps bring new growth into our lives.

CANDLES ARE LIT AT THIS TIME to represent the return of the light as the Sun's energy begins to increase. In Celtic tradition, the Triple Goddess has become her virgin self again, known as Bride, Brigid, Brigit, the Maiden, Keeper of the Sacred Fire. Her attributes are intuition, inspiration, divination, the spark of life. Her life-giving waters are the sacred springs and holy wells of our land, and were honoured at this time. She is the preserver of tradition through poetry and song. In Celtic countries, poetry was understood as channelled ancestral memory. It was seen as sacred, as an aspect of clairvoyance, vision and divination. English, Welsh, Scottish and Irish mythology are rich with legends of the beguiling spring maiden who is called Olwen, Niwalen, Gwenhyver, Blodeuwedd, Brigid, who initiates the young king in a deeply spiritual sexual experience. Hidden in these tales of love and sexual initiation lies the secret alchemy of Imbolc. The fertile power of the young female represents the power of the unconscious and the spark of intuition from within. It joins with the active outer consciousness, represented by the Sun king. It is this union of these two aspects of ourselves and of the energy this creates, which brings new life, growth and manifestation.

Other ancient myths reflect the same process in action. Persephone returns from the Underworld (the inner world) as her self, made new, the young spring maiden.

Before this, she sits in her cave and spins a web of a great picture of the universe that 'the Mother makes into reality'. Northern Europeans worshipped the great goddess Freya, the virgin aspect of the Triple Goddess who, in Nordic myth, is the Three Fates who stood at the foot of Odin's tree of sacrifice. The constellation of Orion was called the distaff of Mary, but previously it was called the distaff of Freya who spun the fates of men (humankind). Freya represents sexual love; her alternative name 'Frigg' became slang for sexual intercourse. Clotho in Greek myth was known as the fate virgin, the fate spinner, the first of the Moerae (later called Mary) who spun the thread of destiny. Roman Pagans worshipped Juno Februata, the goddess of the fever (febris) of love, later replaced with St Valentine by the church. Athene, Isis, Minerva, Diana, Aphrodite – are all similar aspects of this energy.

The early image of the virgin was very different from what we now understand it to be. She was seen as powerful, full of her inherent ability to be fertile. She was honoured for her vibrant sexuality. In pre-Christian Rome, the 'Virgines' were unmarried women. They combined a natural abundant sexuality with the potential of motherhood and procreation. These free young women must have presented as much a threat to the new patriarchal church as the old matriarchs. A marriage system was introduced which harnessed women's natural nurturing caring instincts to serve men. Her sexuality became feared by the church and by men for its potential power over them. To complete the reversal of values, virgin became synonymous with purity.

The worship of the goddess was channelled by the church into the worship of the Virgin Mary. It is interesting that virginity is the most emphasised aspect of her, not her motherhood, even though her virginity was wildly inexplicable. They were well aware that the goddess worship they sought to suppress could re-establish itself through the worship of Mary, so they diffused and debased her power and the power of the female. Mary became passive, meek, subordinate, without sexuality, successfully removing her previous attributes. This complex reversal of women's natural instincts, as a method of control by the church has, of course, had the most dramatic and far-reaching psychological and sociological effects throughout the Christianised patriarchal world. Inner reflection, the unconscious, the intuition, receptivity, and the inner voice – all became synonymous with everything female and was also denied, suppressed and feared. This has meant that men as well as women have been cut off from these vital aspects of themselves.

The church incorporated this festival into their religion as Candlemas, celebrated on the 2nd February. Candlemas became known as the festival of the 'Purification of the Virgin Mary', a time that according to Judaeo-Christian rule, a woman must be purified forty days after childbirth, as she had been made unclean by the event! This removed all previous understanding of the power behind this ancient festival of Candlemas. 'Cande' from the Anglo-Saxon, and 'Candali', 'Kundali' and 'Kundalini'

from the Sanskrit, all bring association with the raising of sexual energy. This is the serpent that rises up the spine in sacred and sexual union, in which the self merges with the infinite. This reflects an understanding of sexuality and pleasure as a deeply spiritual experience. Eros, an older Greek phallic god, and Cupid, the Roman god of erotic love, were worshipped at a time when sexuality was honoured as a primary life force.

In Celtic mythology, Brighidh was an older solar goddess associated with the awakening hibernating serpent that was said to come forth from its hole on Imbolc eve. In Pagan times, serpents were associated with inspiration, aspiration, healing, the phallus, an emblem of life. The paths of Earth energy were called serpent paths and here at Imbolc their energy becomes reactivated and vibrant.

THE UNDERLYING
ENERGY OF IMBOLC

THE DAYS ARE BEGINNING TO LENGTHEN. It is still cold
but buds are forthcoming on the trees. Sap is beginning to rise and
the bulbs are pushing through the Earth. Everywhere there are signs
of the Earth stirring. Our acceptance of winter is giving way to an
urge to move forwards into springtime energy. Now is the time to
prepare inwardly for the changes that will come. Plant your ideas and
leave them to germinate. Bring your visions and inner understandings out
through poetry, song and art. Divination and clairvoyance are potent now as
the link with the dark unconscious is still strong.

At Lammas, opposite Imbolc on the Wheel of the Year, consciousness began
its descent into the inner realms and the dark, to find inner wisdom and
regeneration. Here at Imbolc the unconscious is emerging from the
time of incubation and rest, revitalised, potent and fertile.

Imbolc is the time for initiation and healing, for reclaiming what
has been forgotten. It is a time for invocation of the life force and
working with the dynamics of its potency. Our intuitive flashes and
sparks of inspiration are needed more than ever to complement the active
rational approach that dominates our western life-style. The returning active
phase of the solar year brings with it an opportunity to use our inner Fire, to
unite our dynamic inner power with the fertile edge of the new year's cycle.

We are trying in our own way to live the dreams and visions of a new age,
but we are still bound by our old conditioning and life patterns. We each
carry the seeds of a new vision, of a new way of being. Each time these
visions re-emerge after the incubation period of winter, they are stronger
and we are surer.

Light is Fire
Fire so pure
The Sun is Fire
The Fires of Heaven
purify me

Vince DeCicco

Praying for the Rain

PREPARATIONS FOR IMBOLC

*Wells and Sacred Springs * Divination*
*Brigid's Cross * Snake Sticks * Garden projects*
*Freya * St Valentine*
Personal Shield-Making
*Trees: Rowan * Willow*
*Herbs: Coltsfoot * Ginger Root*

Decide where and when to celebrate Imbolc. Use the rising energy of the
New Moon to enhance new beginnings. Invite friends and ask them to bring
their poems to read, their creative projects to show, a new candle to light,
something for the shrine and food and drink to share.

Create a simple shrine for Imbolc using white and yellow cloths or scarves.
Pick a small vase of early spring flowers, a vase of twigs in bud or some bulbs
in flowerpots. Bring back something from your walks – anything which
suggests the awakening Earth. Light a candle at the centre, as you focus on
your inspirations, aspirations, dreams and visions for the coming season.

Buy plenty of candles for lighting up the space and some special ones for
invocations and wishes.

Make night-light lanterns of dragons and flowers, or the spirit of the new
year. Create a frame of basket makers willow or cane, and cover it with strong
tissue paper, coated with watered-down PVA glue. Weave a place to hold a jam
jar for the night-light, leaving a gap to get new ones in and out. Decide first if
this is free standing or to be carried? Will it hang from a hook or have handles?

Clear out the old and make way for the new. Clear and clean your
space. Give away unwanted possessions along with their associations. Wash
all your crystals and leave them out in the Sun, Moon and rain to recharge.
Re-examine the resolutions you made at the Winter Solstice. Seek clarity and
wisdom to help you find your way.

Make time for meditation, writing poetry, drawing and painting. Create simple new chants and new tunes. Pick up an instrument, even if you think you can't play. Begin simply with three or four repetitive notes and see what words come to you.

Find ways to celebrate and revive women's arts and crafts such as needlework, weaving, beadwork, macrame. Get together and work on a group project such as making a large quilt that can be hung and displayed. Decide on a theme and decide the size of the square everyone must use. Get the children involved and the men, and create something of great inspiration. The squares can be sewn together and backed. Loops can be sewn onto the top enabling the whole thing to be hung from a pole.

Brigid's Cross

Traditionally made to hang on the door or in windows at Imbolc (similar to God's Eyes), and traditionally woven out of grass, straw, rushes or vines. If you are using dried materials, soak them in water first to restore their flexibility. You can also use natural woven wools. These are the most interesting, but children like to use bright colours.

1. Begin by binding two sticks together that are of equal length as in fig (1). Silver birch, willow, or rowan would all be appropriate wood for the symbolism and significance they represent.

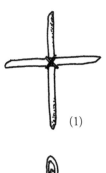
(1)

2. Tie on the first piece of wool, straw etc. Wind it over the first twig, wrapping it round the twig once before moving on to the next twig. Wind it over and round this twig in the same way. Continue round and round in the same pattern, tucking in the ends. These beautiful weavings represent the all-seeing eye of Brigid, to watch over you through the coming year. Shells, beads, tassels or feathers can be hung from it or woven in as you go round. You may try tying three or four sticks together to make them more elaborate and experimental. Old crosses from last year should be ritually burnt to release the old year and open the way to moving forwards.

(2)

Snake Sticks

Another relaxing and focusing activity which can be done alone, with children or a group of friends, is to paint a snake stick, serpent stick or dragon stick. Driftwood is particularly good but any dried stick will do. Check first that it is strong and will not break easily. Chip off some or all of the bark and sandpaper if necessary. You may like to whittle a simple face at one end and tail at the other end and paint patterns on it with acrylic paint.

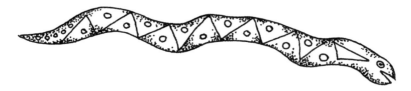

As you work with the image of snake, serpent or dragon, unravel and share what you know and understand about it and any experiences you may have had working with this ancient symbol of power. True to its own nature, it has many layers and levels of energy. Its early pre-Christian meaning of health, healing and potent energy is now resurfacing once again.

Wells and Sacred Springs

Look for any local old wells and sacred springs. They were previously honoured at this time as the lifeblood of the land and worshipped as the source of our well-being. Hellywells and Hels wells as they were known, were associated with the goddess Hellenes, but later they became known as holy wells and became connected to the church. Many fell into disuse and were forgotten, but can sometimes be rediscovered. If you find an old well site, tend and care for it. Plant native spring bulbs and plants around it. Speak out your commitment to restore love and respect to our Earth. Bless and give thanks for pure Water.

Garden Projects

There is still time to plant new trees and bushes and to create magical areas in your garden. Plant a willow archway at the bottom of your garden by cutting willow twigs and planting them straight into the ground. Within a few weeks they will be growing and can eventually be trained and twisted to form a willow archway or a seating area, a place to sit and contemplate. Interweave with honeysuckle, clematis or winter-flowering jasmine. Plant herb seeds indoors now so that you have lots of herbs to plant out when the time comes.

Plan a new outdoor project on your land or in your garden, if you have one. If not, plan a window-ledge project or something to grow outside your door. Let your imagination run wild. Plan to create something unique and inspirational. One big plant pot can become a mini-world with rocks, crystals and wood placed amongst miniature alpine and dwarf varieties of plants. Solar fountains (with a backup system for dull days or night-time) can be used to create a very special place, with a seat nearby, planted with sweet-smelling herbs. Represent each of the Five Elements with appropriate plants, colours. The list is endless. An outdoor project will bring you connection to the Earth both in the doing and the end result, satisfying many aspects and levels of your being.

Write poetry, indulging in your imagination, releasing your hidden or pent-up feelings. Let it all pour out. It doesn't have to be 'polished' or 'finished'. You don't have to show it to anyone or even keep it. Just do it for yourself and see what comes out. If you like it or like some of it, share what you want to with friends or write it in a special book. Above all, you will find understanding and your own wisdom hidden within it. From your unconscious many things will be revealed to help your understanding of yourself. Bringing things out from the unconscious is the special energy of Imbolc and may help you to find your way forward.

Freya

A great goddess of Northern Europe who represented sexual erotic love. Her sacred day was Friday and was considered to be the best day for weddings. The Romans re-named this day 'dies Veneris' after Venus, their own version of this goddess. In pre-Christian times, Friday was a holy day dedicated to Freya. Fish were eaten as symbols of fertility. Later, of course, Friday was called 'unlucky' and doubly unlucky if it fell on the 13th as it combined the goddess' sacred number (the number of lunar months in a year) and her sacred day.

St Valentine

February has long associations with sexuality and love. Juno Februata, the Roman goddess of love, gave her name to the month, and the festival of Luperealia on the ides of February included a tradition of exchanging small papers or 'billets' on which partners were chosen for erotic games. These forerunners of our valentine cards were discouraged by the church who tried to replace them with short sermons. But the love notes survived, although changed from their original meaning. The church replaced Juno Februata with St Valentine, a mythical martyr who was said to be executed at the very moment he received his billet of love from his sweetheart. Despite all efforts of the church, this festival remains dedicated to lovers. Eros, Cupid, Kama, Priapus and

Pan are all gods of erotic love from Pagan times when sexuality as a primary life force was worshipped – Renaissance art depicted Cupid as a small winged baby, but ancient talismans of Cupid were winged phalli made in bronze, bone and wood. Cupid was the son of Venus and Mercury, the 'Goddess of Love' and a god of communication between the worlds and serpent energy (in Greek myth Aphrodite and Hermes). Their child Eros, a god of erotic love, was an 'hermaphrodite', combining both the male and female qualities of these two deities.

Explore and research serpents and dragons. Two serpents entwined around a central rod is a pre-Christian symbol, which represents physical and spiritual health, as in the Greek caduceus. The double spiral or double serpent represents the genetic double helix, the DNA. The serpent was seen as an emblem of the life force, intrinsically linked to the power of sexuality, the phallus and inner wisdom.

Begin a Moon diary. Working with the cycles of the Moon brings a deeper understanding of the duality of light (waxing Moon) and dark (waning Moon). The Moon puts us in touch with our emotional receptivity and unconscious selves. Receptivity is a state of attentive listening, focusing inward rather than giving out. It means being tuned in to your self, ready to receive inspiration from within. This will help balance our over emphasis on rational and logical thinking.

Personal Shield Making

Make a personal shield to hang in your sacred space. The Celts would have used their shields to identify themselves through a symbol of power, an outer representation of the inner spiritual warrior. The making of a shield will help to bring the inner and outer person into a balanced whole. It is also a way of connecting to the rich layers of symbolism that have been handed down to us through the ages from the many multi-cultural roots that are our heritage. Choose the symbols you feel a close affinity to, such as animal and bird totems, symbols of power and wisdom, symbols of balance and held energy, symbols of healing and clan affinity.

1. Begin by making a hoop from a freshly cut straight hazel rod. Bind the two ends together with strong garden twine or leather, and leave to dry out for a week or two so that the wood can shrink. You may add strength to the frame by binding on a cross of cut hazel (1). The hoop frame can be bound in strips of chamois leather or wool or gently sanded with a fine sandpaper and oil to bring out the colours of the wood.

2. Traditionally the hoop would have been covered in a piece of hide. Chamois leather works well, or cotton, sailcloth, or calico. Make holes around the edge at regular intervals and thread a length of twine or leather thong through them. This pulls the material or hide tightly round the frame. Knot firmly (2).

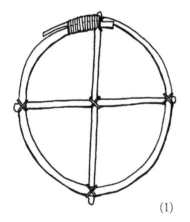

(1)

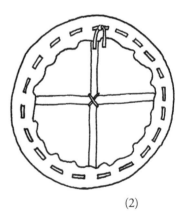

(2)

3. An alternative method is to use strong twine or leather to lash in the central material. Material needs to be turned in and sewn to make the edge strong (3). Don't worry about making a perfect circle. It is the process that is important and your technique will improve with practice.

4. Meditate on what images you wish to depict. Make drawings on paper and then decide on your background colour. Paint the cotton material with emulsion or acrylic paint. This stiffens it up a bit and provides a good base on which to paint your design. Acrylics are permanent and waterproof; if you are using a piece of hide, paint directly onto the hide. Create a power song as you work and breathe life into your ceremonial power shield.

5. Alternatively, sew your design on, using different materials (appliqué). Buy a large circular embroidery frame; it will help keep your material taut as you sew. Using a free style stitch, embroider the images and colours you want to depict. This can then be put into the hazel hoop by any of the methods described.

(4)

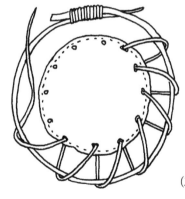

(3)

TREES OF IMBOLC

ROWAN – *Sorbus aucuparia*

Rowan is the second tree of the Celtic Tree Ogham: LUIS. L. It has long associations with the Maiden aspect of the Triple Goddess, is ruled by Mercury, the principle of communication between the worlds and is also associated with serpents. Rowan is also known as Quickbeam or the Quickening tree. It will help 'quicken' your psychic abilities and connections. It has a beneficial protective energy that will help increase your abilities to receive visions and insights and will help increase communication with the spirit realms.

Spending time with the rowan will strengthen your positive life force energy so that your personal power is so strong it can withstand any negative influences. This is why in the past it was used for protection and to ward off evil. Sprays of leaves were hung in doorways, worn in the hat or carried as a talisman.

Rune staves, the sticks on which Runes or Ogham symbols were inscribed, were traditionally made of rowan wood. A rowan wand will enhance clairvoyance; bringing greater clarity in interpreting the messages we may receive. A rowan walking stick is particularly potent and is good for night walking.

Plant a rowan tree near your house or by your gate. This small beautiful tree is ideal in a garden. It has starry white flowers in the spring, sparse light foliage in the summer, and the leaves turn bright red and orange in the autumn along with abundant clusters of bright red berries which attract the birds. The berries can be used for sore throats and hoarseness and as a mild laxative. They can also be made into a jelly (jam) by mixing them with crab apples and also made into wine.

Make a Rowan Wand, Touchwood or Walking Stick

Look for a straight length of rowan wood to use and ask the tree before cutting.
Respect the tree at all times. Thank the tree for its gift. Take the bark off as soon as
possible, if you want to get down to the wood. When it is stripped, leave the wood to
dry out somewhere cool but inside, to preserve the colour of the wood. After it has
dried out, carve it and sand it using rough sandpaper first, then medium, then fine.
It is a beautiful wood to carve. Lastly, oil it to preserve the wood.

WILLOW – *Salix alba/Salix nigra*

This is the fourth tree in the Celtic Tree Ogham: SAILLE. S. It also has long associated
with the Maid aspect of the Triple Goddess. The word saille became anglicised from
the Latin *'salire'* – to leap, and old French 'saille' meaning to rush out suddenly. This
became 'sally' meaning a sudden outburst of emotions, action or expression, as in 'sally
forth'. It is a quick growing tree that roots easily from freshly cut twigs.

Known in Celtic myth and folklore as a tree of enchantment and
dreaming, it was associated with poets, the Moon and Water. It greatly
enhances confidence to follow your intuition and inspired leaps of the
imagination; it puts you in touch with your feelings and deeply buried
emotions. The willow helps us to express these, letting them out and
owning them. The twigs of the willow are flexible, teaching us to move
with life rather than resist what we are feeling.

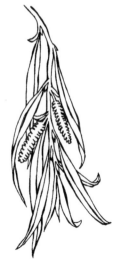

The willow's essential energy is this power
to help things move from the unconscious
level to the conscious level. Whether you are
over-stimulated by your feelings or cut off from
them, spending time with a willow tree will help
heal the imbalance. Taking the flower essence
will help in the same way. It has long been used
as a symbol of grief and those who have been forsaken in love.
Deserted lovers would wear 'the green willow' to share their
heartache with others. Our deep unconscious thoughts speak to
us through our dreams. Sleep with a willow wand under your
pillow to encourage your dreams to surface and for assimilating
inspired or ancient teachings. Freshly cut willow whips are used
for binding magical and sacred objects.

HERBS OF IMBOLC

COLTSFOOT – *Tussilago farfara*

In February the coltsfoot flowers appear before the
large leaves that come later. *'Lago'* in Latin means
'I carry' (away) and holds a clue to its inherent
energy of moving emotional and physical
stagnation. It is a primary lung remedy, expelling
phlegm from the lungs and easing irritating
coughs. It will also help expel tar, dust and other
pollutants from the lungs. Previously the flowers and
leaves were the main component of 'country tobacco',
which can be safely smoked and impart the herbal properties already listed. The flowers
and leaves can be made into herbal tea. Pour half a litre of boiling water onto a handful
of the dried herb and mix in some fresh flowers if you have them. Cover and leave for
ten minutes. Drink a wineglassful three times a day. Keep in the fridge and drink cold
or gently re-heat, but do not boil. Add honey. Drink to relieve any lung congestion,
coughs, asthma, drink after walking or cycling in traffic. Drink or burn as an incense,
to clear energy, inspire vision and create clarity.

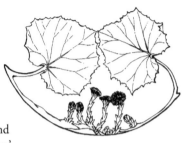

GINGER ROOT – *Zingiber officinale*

Ginger has long been associated with dragons. A good herb for this time of year as
it will help revitalise and stimulate the Fire within. Use where the cold and damp of
winter has caused problems such as head colds, catarrh, poor circulation, chilblains,
digestive sluggishness, menstrual cramps, and for people who continually feel the cold.
Use whenever you need to increase Fire in the body and get things moving.

Bring 50g of ginger root, the thinly peeled rind of a lemon and half a litre of water to
the boil, and gently simmer for half an hour or so. Strain and when cold keep in the
fridge. Add 1tbsp of this liquid to a cup of hot water and sweeten with honey. Drink as
needed.

**Warning: Do not use if there is high blood pressure, stomach ulcers
or inflammatory bowel conditions, as it will aggravate them.**

IMBOLC CELEBRATIONS

These are some suggestions for celebrating Imbolc.

Spend time outside, feeling the emergence of the life force. Talk to the trees, welcome the awakening dryads and nature spirits. Pick some snowdrops and other early spring flowers for your Imbolc shrine. Cut some twigs of willow, dogwood, forsythia, winter jasmine, almond and cherry blossom. Weave them into a circle the same as you did with the Winter Solstice wreath, but this time place it in a wide shallow bowl of water. Keep the water topped up and during the next few weeks the twigs will begin to root and the leaves and blossom will come out. Place moss, a stone or a crystal in the centre of the circle and leave on a window ledge. Arrange any twigs left over into a vase of water. If gathering with friends, this could be something you make together at the beginning or the end of the celebration.

Place on the shrine any methods of divination you may wish to use, such as Ogham sticks, Tarot cards, Runes, or I Ching. Now is a good time to use any of these systems to help you see the way forward.

Burn dried coltsfoot as an incense, or drink as a tea to help focus and clear channels so that your intuition and inspiration will flow.

Put aside a special day and evening to spend by yourself or with friends. Keep your focus on your intuition and inner voice. Let your rational mind go, follow what you 'feel' is right and not what you 'think', 'ought' or 'should'.

It is good to have a fire outside if the weather is fine. Failing that, find creative ways to light your celebration space with candles to celebrate the return of the light and the kindling of the inner Fire. Symbolically cleanse and purify by Fire what you wish to clear away and leave behind. You could write this down on a piece of paper to burn in a ritual fire, visualising it being transformed. Saying, "I clear away..." or "I leave behind..." gives it added power.

Burn dried sage and use the smoke to cleanse each other's aura or spirit body, which exists around the physical one. This is a Native American tradition, but it has become very popular in ceremonies here. Waft the smoke with a large feather or bird's wing, if you have one.

Welcome and thank the Five Elements as part of your opening ceremony.
Gather the group together in a circle. If you are on your own, sit or stand inside the circle with the directions either around you or lain out before you on a circular tray. Say what spontaneously comes to you and helps you and those gathered to focus.

Earth in the North
Give thanks for Earth, her beauty and all that you love about this time of year. Welcome the rising life force, which is now potent again. Give thanks for the seeds beginning to stir and germinate. Activate the seeds of your hopes and wishes, of future actions and that which you wish to manifest. Welcome the nature spirits waking from their long winter sleep and all aspects of nature as it begins to stir. Welcome the serpent or dragon force of the land as it awakes.

Air in the East
Celebrate your intuition, inspiration, the unconscious, clairvoyance, messages from dreams and the spirit realms. Give thanks for your visions that have come to you as you daydream or stare into space. This is the time of new beginnings, new ideas, new directions and of communication from within. Celebrate your muse, your poetry, your voice, and all you communicate to the world.

Fire in the South
Thank Fire as it emerges now. Light the inner Fire. Rebirth the Spirit into the conscious realms and notice the upsurge in personal energy this brings. This is the time for sparking the life force, for the spark of sexuality and the potential of love. Give thanks for this. This is the time for release, initiation, expansion, transformation, creativity and dynamic expressive power. Give thanks for your imagination, the spark of the creative life force from within.

Water in the West
Give thanks for the Water that gives us life. May our actions be guided by the reflective, feeling, nurturing side of ourselves – the path of the heart. May we

remember to be guided by our love, to follow our dreams and deepest wishes, and to seek out the things that need healing.

Spirit at the Centre

Within and without and ever present. We give thanks for this vital connection to this essential part of ourselves that cannot be seen and cannot be named. We reach out and in, connecting to our source and to guidance from within. We touch the sacred, the still point of power at the centre of our being. Through it we are a part of all life and all existence on this Earth.

The words I have written here are intended as clues, and pathways to understanding. When invoking the elements, it is important to speak from the heart and with power, so that you help to make the connection strong for yourself and all those present. Use the elemental charts on pages 30-34 to help you.

Spend time in meditation. Reach out and feel the stirrings of the Earth and seek oneness with the germinating seeds deep within the still cold ground. Ask for guidance to help you move forwards, and for directions which will serve your greater good and the healing of the Earth. Meditate on your reflective intuitive qualities and how you can use them and enhance them in your life.

Pass around seeds or crystals and each imagine what you wish to grow. Later plant the seeds or bury the crystals. Speak in the present tense and imagine it is already on its way.

Each light a candle for the positive qualities you value about yourself. Share these with each other and how you hope to use these in the coming active phase of the year's cycle. Plant the candles in a large bowl of earth or sand in the centre of the circle and let them burn right down.

Light candles for those you love and their positive qualities you value. Light candles for healing, for friends, family and yourself. Light candles for the Earth. Light candles to celebrate the activation of the inner Fire, for the Fire of inspiration, for illumination, for the spark of sexuality and attraction.

Symbolically clear away the dross and dormancy of winter. Cleanse and purify what you wish to leave behind by writing words on paper and give them to the flames to transform.

Make a pledge to honour and listen to your intuition, your inner voice, your inner wisdom. These inner qualities are vital links to our spirituality and understanding of ourselves. The beginning of this new journey of discovery and joy lies here with your pledge.

Release yourself from the fear, the superstitions and old patterns that might be controlling your emotions, inner consciousness and spiritual well-being. Name what you think they are and let them go.

Many folk dances still follow the retrograde motion of the Moon (widdershins) instead of the clockwise motion of the Sun. The church reversed the directions of all circular walks, i.e. around boundaries and wells, as well as charms. Explore the energy inherent within Sun-wise or Moon-wise rituals.

Chanting or toning enhances power, energises the body and stills the mind. Incantation is a means of gathering energy from within. Enchant comes from 'incantre', to sing over, and women's singing was particularly feared for its power to charm. The use of chanting or toning in ritual helps to bring altered states of mind, opening the way into and out of the inner realms. The chant should consist of a short memorable phrase. It is better if it is no more than two or three lines long. It is repeated over and over again until the energy and power have built up and shifted on to another level of consciousness. Bring in harmonies, experiment, be creative and spontaneous!

Ritually burn the evergreens that were brought into the house for Winter Solstice. Give thanks. Scatter the ashes under the fruit trees.

What are the seeds of your future that you wish to germinate and see grow? Write them on curls of silver birch bark, or slips of paper that can be rolled up into a scroll, to represent your new beginnings. Wrap them in coloured threads and hang them up by threading them onto embroidery thread with a large strong needle. Tie them to birch trees or hang them from birch twigs and hang in the window.

Rites of Passage

Imbolc is a time for transformation and change. Create rites of passage for each other so that we can move on from old outworn ideas, attitudes and parts of our lives that no longer are helpful to us and reintegrate into new patterns and ways of being which will serve us better. A rite of passage has three parts to it. The first part is separation from the old, what you want to leave behind. The second is the place of transition, such as a doorway, archway, something to step over, under or through, and the third is integration into the new. Help each other create a simple affirmation or statement of intent for the third part. This is spoken in the present tense and can be repeated daily to help strengthen the new way forward.

Share with each other the poems, chants, music and songs you have been creating. Inspire each other with your visions and creativity. Share with each other your accomplishments of all kinds, celebrating the re-emergence of the self as you step out into the active phase of the year.

Sit together and make wands of willow or rowan. Both will help you make a connection to your intuition and unconscious. The twigs should be cut with the blessing of the tree at least two weeks before you need them, to give them a chance to dry out a bit. Peel off the bark, shape the ends, carve if you wish, and then sandpaper, beginning with rough, then medium, then fine.

Weave circles of fresh willow whips to wear on your head, to signify and amplify being in touch with your emotions. Look for ways to help your self deal with your feelings and emotions. How can you bring them out in positive expressive ways? Share these thoughts with each other. Drinking sage tea will help release stagnant emotions. Sage works on the throat and will help to release emotion through the use of sound. Let out how you feel. Let it all out and express yourself. Vocalise!

Dance together in a circle or on your own. Weave into the dance everything you wish to change, what you want to begin and transform in your life. Weave new dreams to take hold and grow. This is the spark of power that initiates their becoming. Dance to celebrate being free of winter. Dance to be free of old outworn restrictions. Release words of invocation for a new direction. Dance to activate the Fire within. Dance to release negative attachments. Dance to let go of the old and embrace the new. Dance your dreams awake!

Bring the group together for a closing ceremony by holding hands in a circle. If you are on your own, come into your centre and stillness. Thank the guardians, angels and spirit guides, for their presence and help. Thank each of the elements for their guidance and thank each other. End on a chant that carries forward the energy of Imbolc in everyone's heart - something to take with you into daily life, to remind and connect you to the sacred in yourself.

Bless the food and drink to share.

SPRING EQUINOX

SPRING QUARTER POINT
21st - 22nd March

SUN ENTERS ARIES ♈

Day and night equal length

*Oestre * Eostre * Eostar*
*Ostara * Easter*

The Festival of Awakening
The Festival of Balance
The Festival of New Life
The first day of Spring

SPRING EQUINOX

Day and night are of equal length all over the
world. In the northern hemisphere we still
celebrate it as the first day of spring. The days
are getting longer and warmer now, and the
nights shorter. This is the festival of balance:
the balance of light and dark, the balance
of the inner world and the outer world, the
balance and joining of the conscious and
the unconscious. Here at the Equinox, we can
look at and work towards this balance within
ourselves. This will bring change and healing as we
move forwards to new understandings and ways of living
from this perspective.

THE CELTS UNDERSTOOD THAT the physical, mental and spiritual levels were so
interlocked and perfectly balanced, that whatever is done on one level will inevitably
affect the other two. We do nothing in isolation. Your spiritual understanding
constantly affects your decisions in your everyday life. Your thoughts and your
emotions affect your spirit, your health and what you attract into your life. Here at
Equinox, make time to understand this balanced flow of energy we are part of.

Spring Equinox is often symbolised by a beguiling spring maiden with a basket
of eggs. The female is represented because from her new life comes. The egg symbolises
the rebirth of nature, the fertility of the Earth and creation. The egg is potential life,
full of promise. The cosmic egg contains male and female, light and dark, expansion
and contraction, conscious and unconscious, continuity and balance. The plans that
have been incubating on the inner levels since the autumn can now hatch out onto
the physical plane. Both the Spring and the Autumn Equinoxes have a long history of
dragons. Here at the Spring Equinox the dragon energies, both within the Earth and
ourselves, are waking up.

Oestre, the 'Goddess of Light', brings fertility with the spring. This is the root of the
word 'oestrus', the time in an animal's sexual cycle when it is fertile when the hormone

oestrogen is stimulating ovulation. The church overlaid this festival with Easter and its theme of rebirth and resurrection from death. Easter is still based on the old lunar calendar: the first Sunday after the first Full Moon after the Spring Equinox, formerly the pregnant phase of Oestre passing into the fertile season.

The Pagan tradition celebrates the union of the beautiful spring maiden with the young ardent male. Their union makes all of nature fertile. Here we can make contact with their archetypal energy within ourselves, no matter what our age or gender. Many women are now seeking to balance their male and female sides within themselves and are looking for the same balance in men. The ardent young man, who is non-aggressive, in touch with his instincts and can show his feelings, is a precious image to hold. The Greeks gave us Pan with horns and hooves, part man, part animal. The Celts gave us Cernunnos or Herne, also with horns, in touch with his animal instincts, wise, magical, the master of the three levels of existence, playful, sexual, sensuous, spiritual. He was outlawed by the church who changed him into the devil, the root of evil, thereby denying men an essential part of themselves. We need to reclaim him. Men need to connect to his life-giving instinctive nature. Women need to find him in the men they know. Here lies the spark, the power in their joining and their joint potential that will change the future.

Beyond this, we need to balance these energies within ourselves regardless of gender. The union of the rational conscious mind when joined with the intuition and inner wisdom brings fertility and new life on many levels. We can consciously make new things fertile by what we choose to bring together, by what we give our energy and attention to. Whatever we give our attention to will grow.

Make it your intention to balance your rational logical mind with your intuitive feeling self. Learn to listen to your inner voice, to trust and act on your inner wisdom, your intuition and your instincts, and bring your whole self back into balance.

THE UNDERLYING ENERGY OF SPRING EQUINOX

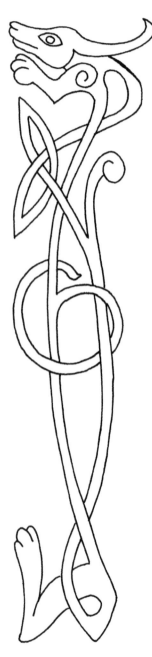

EVERYTHING IN NATURE IS coming alive and awakening. The Sun is gaining strength; the days are longer and warmer. Blossom and catkins are on the trees, buds are bursting, seeds are germinating, spring flowers appear, eggs are hatching and all the animals are preparing to have their young. Everywhere is evidence of life's ability to regenerate.

The Earth is turning from the dark depths of winter to an outward manifestation and expression of the new outer growth cycle. It is time to throw off the restraints of winter and reach out for what it is we want for the world and ourselves.

It is a time of rain and sunshine, the mingling of the elements of Fire and Water, spring gales, high tides, feelings of wildness and chaos. Run wild in the wind and celebrate life's fertility. It is a time to begin new ventures, make plans, journey. Celebrate breaking out and moving forwards. Feel empowered to take risks, strike out on your own and make things happen.

Bring opposite forces into balance: light with dark, conscious with unconscious, Fire with Water. Here is the union of power that brings fertility and manifestation. This is the spark of the life force, the dance of life – interdependent complementary parts of one energy system which we can embrace on our journey to become whole.

I am the hare
of Eostre
I am the sweet maiden's messenger
I am springing over the fresh green shoots
Look at me run in exhalation
Sun shines brightly
Solar power ascends
Sap rises urging creation
Surging power, flowing...
growing...

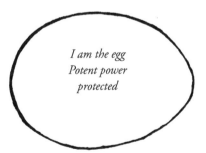

I am the egg
Potent power
protected

Nicky Martin

PREPARATIONS FOR SPRING EQUINOX

*Decorated Eggs * Making Flags*
*Symbols of Balance * Dragons*
*Making a Dragon * Things to Fly in the Wind*
Trees: Ash and Alder
*Herbs: Nettle * Cleavers * Hyssop*

Celebrate with friends or on your own (or both) and decide where you might go to enhance your connection to Earth energies – a place where you can make contact with newly awakening nature, commune with the trees and feel the pulse of the Earth as it hums with new life.

Create a shrine that reflects your spiritual and sacred connections.
It may be in a room, in the garden or out on the land. Bring together things which will help you focus on balance, awakening and new life. This is a very uplifting and peaceful thing to do and will bring a sense of direction as you work. Perfectly in harmony with the time, you actively bring out into the world what you are connected to within. Sing while you create, and see what insights this may bring. This could provide inspiration for a chant for your celebration and ceremony.

If you already have a shrine, then give everything a spring clean and a change-around. Clear out your five elemental areas in the garden. Re-plan, re-plant, activate the energy, manifest the new understandings and insights you have gained during the winter's incubation period.

Plant new seeds of herbs and native plants, especially those that you can dry in the later months for ceremony, medicine and cooking.

Decorate Hen's Eggs

Hardboiled eggs are easiest for young children. Paint them with acrylics or felt tip pens. Blown eggs can be hung in the window or used as part of your Spring Equinox shrine. To blow an egg, simply make a hole with a pin at each end, and blow the contents out through the other. Blown eggs can be decorated by dipping them in coloured candle wax and scratching off a pattern; by glueing on straw, string or coloured threads or wool to them. Blown eggs can be hung up by tying a piece of string to half a matchstick, then sliding it into the hole at the top to wedge against the inside of the egg. Alternatively, tie a bead to a piece of thread and thread through the egg with a long needle so the bead is at the bottom. There are many traditional folk designs to be found in countries all over Europe along with many customs concerning eggs at this time.

Flags

Make flags to fly in the wind, to carry your prayers and your wishes – flags of vision, flags with symbols to invoke and carry energy. There are many different shapes and ways to do this.

Long prayer flags: Use cotton or organza and paint on images with fabric paint. Attach to six-foot hazel or ash poles and embed in the earth.

Flags to carry or hang from a window: The pole will need to be shorter according to its use and the size of the person carrying it.

Ribbons on Sticks

Tape or bind a loop of ribbon to the top of a stick and then thread a long length of ribbon through the loop and sew the end (see illustration). This can be whirled around and danced with.

SYMBOLS OF BALANCE

Celtic Cross

This symbol is common to almost every shamanic tradition in the world and appears on stones throughout the Celtic lands. It represents the natural order: the two Equinoxes crossed by the two Solstices, the four seasons, the four directions and the Five Elements of life. The centre and the circumference represent the fifth element, Spirit, the cycle of life and the circle of existence.

Entwined Serpent

This represents the balancing of the self and the awareness of the male and female energies that exist within each person.

The Caduceus

This is the symbol of the homeopathic medical profession, healing, alchemy, and Hermes/Mercury. It symbolises the volatile and fixed principles: mercury and sulphur, male and female, light and dark.

The Spiral

This symbolises unfolding growth within and without; spirit into matter and matter into spirit ascending and descending. At the centre is the place of perfect balance.

Six Pointed Star

Originating in Tantric Hinduism and adopted as a Judaic symbol. The downward pointing triangle is the alchemical symbol for Water. The upward pointing triangle is the alchemical symbol for Fire. The union of Fire and Water, conscious and unconscious is a path to inner peace and balance.

Triple Spiral or Triskelion

This represents the three circles of existence and everlasting life; The Triple Goddess; Maid, Mother and Crone; Spiritual, mental and physical; Past, present and future.

Yin and Yang
Chinese symbol of light
and dark, male and female,
Sun and Moon. Each side
contains the seed of the
other. Balance. Harmony.

A similar pattern
found on standing
stones and in
Celtic design.

DRAGONS

DRAGON DAY WAS CELEBRATED twice yearly at the Equinoxes. Dragon images
were paraded through the streets and symbolically killed or staked in fertility and
Earth-stimulating rituals and celebrations. Many processions had a St George whose
name means 'tiller of the Earth'. He may, in fact, have been a geomancer rather than a
dragon-slayer. St Michael was the church's champion for destroying dragons, an action
that seems to be synonymous with destroying the old religion. Some dragon paths or
paths of Earth energy can be traced by following St Michael's churches which were
built on hilltops over sacred sites of the old religion and sites dedicated to Mercury or
Hermes.

The ancient track ways, the ridgeways, were said to be the backbone of the dragon.
The ancient burial mounds were known as dragon hills and said to be guarded by
dragons. These mounds are built over areas of intense underground radiation. The
energy of the dragon paths meanders from side to side (sometimes called the Mary
line as its path follows churches dedicated to St Mary, springs, wells, and other places
associated with the female principle). But the straight line of the leyline or St Michael
line seems to direct the energy from point to point across the landscape.

It is now beginning to be understood that in the past the dragon wasn't killed but
staked, and that this may have been a form of Earth acupuncture such as is practised
today by modern dowsers who can detect black radiation, black streams or black water.
These are found directly above certain underground water-bearing fissures and badly
affect the health of the people, animals and crops who live above them. Modern-day
dowsers redirect this harmful energy by 'staking' it with copper pipes. Thus the Earth
energy is controlled and re-balanced in areas where it has become stuck or 'poisoned'
(the noxious breath of the dragon), and the local geomancer sorts it out, sword (stake)
in hand.

From Spring Equinox to St George's Day (23rd April, almost Beltain) many
dragon rituals and processions took place. The fertile Earth energy is activated and
runs strongly through the land. Spring was given a good welcome in with music and
dancing in the streets. It is said that Druids made a journey to the seashore to look

for the red egg of the serpent that symbolised the entry of the seed or germ of life into the Earth.

Higher vital energy is sometimes called dragon fire. This comes from spiritual devotion and can be seen as a flame burning brightly from within. It has been found that the pineal gland, when stimulated by natural sunlight (not artificial light), will bring a natural enthusiasm akin to a spiritual connection. The more time you spend outside with nature, the more you consciously connect to your spiritual path, the more enthusiasm you will draw into your life.

Processions, Theatre and Dragon Making

Theatre, plays or dance theatre can be prepared to perform at the Equinox. Include a dragon procession at the beginning or at the end in the age-old folk tradition of Equinox. Making the dragon is of course quite a big undertaking and could be done as a group project.

1. Make a shape of a dragon's head with basket maker's willow or cane. Use masking tape to secure the places where several whips cross each other, and to bind over the joins. Cover the whole thing with torn strips of cotton sheeting dipped in watered-down PVA glue; or several layers of torn newspaper, also soaked in PVA. When this is dry, paint and decorate in all its splendour. Red, black and gold are traditional dragon colours.

2. Alternatively use a cardboard box as a base for the head, cutting and shaping it, and using paper masking tape to add other cardboard-shaped pieces for nostrils etc. Cover with material or paper that has been soaked in PVA and mould it around the shapes underneath. Paint with emulsion and when dry, decorate with coloured material or paint.

3. The body is joined on to the top of the head and can be made using a series of willow or hazel hoops to which a long piece of material is attached. The head will need one or two people to carry it and each hoop of the body will need one person.

4. Wings can be made using a piece of hazel or willow to which fabric has been attached. Two people inside the 'body' can each carry a wing.

TREES OF SPRING EQUINOX

ASH – *Faxinus excelsior*

The ash is the fifth tree of the Celtic Tree Ogham: NION. N. and is associated with understanding universal truths. It appears in Norse mythology as Yggdrasil, the Great Ash of Odin or Woden who hung from it to obtain enlightenment and the secret of the Runes. Ash teaches us that all of life is interconnected on all levels of existence – past, present and future, spiritual, mental and physical. Whatever happens on one level happens on all levels. Your actions and your thoughts form an endless chain of events and whatever you do in the physical world will affect all levels of your being.

Due to its straightness of growth, it is an excellent wood for making walking sticks and staffs. It carves easily. In woods where it grows with honeysuckle, it is possible to find sticks that have been spiralled by the honeysuckle binds. These are particularly potent for wands and talking sticks.

ALDER – *Alnus glutinosa*

The alder grows alongside rivers where it can be seen easily in the spring as it shimmers in a red haze formed by its reddish brown catkins. It is the third tree of the Celtic Tree Ogham: FEARN. F. and it represents the balance of Fire and Water. It brings a powerful direct energy which will help you to take up challenges and face things previously avoided, balanced with a receptive understanding and awareness of what is going on below the surface. Spending time with the alder will help you to know when to move forward with courage and strength, challenging everything which doesn't ring true, and when to find inner stillness and receptivity to divine inspiration. These are the challenges of a spiritual warrior.

Alder leaves are cooling and soothing and can be pulped to form a poultice for sores and swellings. Use the fresh leaves inside your boots to soothe aching or burning feet when travelling long distances. Alder yields three powerful dyes: the catkins make a strong green dye, associated with the outlaws and foresters in medieval times and faerie's clothes (to keep them hidden from humans). The bark yields a red dye, used by the Celts, and the twigs yield a brown dye. The wood is oily and water-resistant – good for outdoor use, will resist damp or wet. It is easy to carve by hand.

117

HERBS OF SPRING EQUINOX

NETTLE – *Urtica dioica and Urtica urens*
A famed spring tonic. Regular cups of nettle tea will tone up the
whole system and cleanse the blood. Use the nettle tops in soup or
as a vegetable (once cooked, it loses its sting). It is rich in iron.
Nettle has a fiery energy so drink every day to break free of
stagnant emotional states and to contact the warrior within.
Pour boiling water over the fresh plant and
drink frequently.

CLEAVERS – *Galium aparine*
Cleavers is a prime blood purifying herb and an
important spring tonic. It was added to beer in the
spring. Pour boiling water over a few sprigs of the fresh
plant and cover. Leave to infuse for ten minutes. Strain
off the herb. Drink as a daily tonic. It is nice cold so keep
the infusion in the fridge and drink with ice and lemon.
Eat in salad.

HYSSOP – *Hyssopus officinalis*
Hyssop is a herb of purification previously used for cleansing temples and holy places.
It can be used for washing all your special things on your shrine or sacred space. It has
an association with dragons and serpents and the raising of the kundalini from the
base of the spine. It will help balance the emotions. Drink as a tea, burn as an incense
or throw on ritual fires. It is a blood cleanser, cleansing lung remedy and liver tonic
and will help build up the system after illness. It is a herb of Jupiter, warming and
strengthening.

SPRING EQUINOX CELEBRATIONS

These are some suggestions for celebrating Spring Equinox

Be outside today, wrap up warm if it is cold, enjoy the elements, the wind and the rain and the sunshine. Rejoice in them! Celebrate the end of winter. Be a mad March hare, run wild and be expansive. Look for the arrival of spring everywhere.

Whether you are celebrating with friends or on your own, choose a wild and powerful place to go today, somewhere where the Earth's energy runs strong, where the serpent or dragon paths can be felt. Experiment with your ability to dowse these energies with a dowsing rod, forked hazel stick or pendulum.

Share a special breakfast outside with friends. Gather somewhere special and spend the day outside.

Make a shrine to honour the awakening Earth with cloths of yellow and green. Place on it spring flowers, early blossom, catkins and pussy willow. Represent the Five Elements in ways that reflect the Equinox.

Meditate with the trees, especially if a particular tree draws you towards it. Put your back against its trunk, feel its life force energy, and be open to receiving impressions and inner understanding from the tree. Hang coloured ribbons in the trees to honour them and celebrate them.

If you are gathered with a group, begin by making a circle holding hands and then walk a spiral inwards to the centre, chanting an easy meditative walking chant. When you get to the centre and are tight together, share your awareness, understanding and feelings: 'May the Spring Equinox bring...' When this has reached its natural end and all has been said, take up each other's hands (be sure to hold the same hand) and the chant, and the person leading the spiral turns its direction outwards again to bring the group back into a circle. (See page 80.)

The group can be led to honour the Five Elements. If outside, mark them with coloured ribbons on sticks pushed into the ground or a stone for each.

Air in the East
Give thanks for the return of spring, unions of all kinds, life renewal, birth, the sounds of birds and song, dawn, inspiration, smells, the breath of life, the balance of light and dark, clouds, spirals, awakening, communication, inner wisdom, the balance of conscious and unconscious.

Fire in the South
Give thanks for expansion, new growth, spontaneity, sexuality, dragon and serpent energy, balanced power, transformation, the Sun, fertility on many levels, Fire within, Fire without, expression, movement.

Water in the West
Give thanks for the life-giving waters of the land, for receptivity, compassion, caring, nurturing, balancing emotions, inner knowing, trusting the intuition, mysticism, enchantment, dreams, poetry, cleansing, following your heart, love, flowing, our deep longings and all that you have been nurturing.

Earth in the North
Give thanks for the Earth Mother, Gaia, for the gifts of the Earth, fertility, abundance of growth, spring flowers, eggs, seeds, germination, roots, buds, shoots, nature spirits, faerie, the green man, Earth energy, dragon and serpent paths, herbs for medicine, manifestation.

Spirit at the Centre
Give thanks for Spirit, for unconditional Love and for this essential part of ourselves. Reach out and in, connecting to your source and the guidance from within. Touch the sacred, the still point of power at the centre of your being. Feel yourself part of all life and all existence.

The words I have written here are intended as clues, and pathways to understanding. When invoking the elements, it is important to speak from the heart and with power, so that you help to make the connection strong for yourself and all those present. Use the elemental charts on pages 30-34 to help you.

Seed Meditation for Renewal and Self-healing

Imagine you are a seed full of life. Plant the seed of yourself in the warm Earth and water it gently until it begins to open. Feel your roots growing and reaching down into the Earth, drinking all the nutrients. Feel the shoot unfold into the air, your leaves unfold soaking up the Sun's rays. All that you need is given - for growing, for your well-being. Picture yourself in radiant health.

Plant the seeds of yourself and look at where you are going now. Affirm your most positive wishes. Connect to your life force. Ask your spirit guides and helpers for direction and remain open to receiving answers from unexpected places.

Honour the Earth and the fertility of all life, the animals, the birds, fish and the insect world, the great abundance of plants and flowers, the herbs for medicine, and all the food growing for us to eat. Honour the balance of the Sun and the Moon, the male and the female, and the power of their union.

Pass an imaginary egg around the circle, each focusing on what they have been incubating since the autumn and wish to bring out into the world. This is the fertile time. Being aware of your direction will greatly enhance the outcome. Share your thoughts with each other if you want to, before passing the egg to the next person. At the end, place the imaginary egg on the shrine.

Fertility will begin to manifest on many levels, through whatever project you undertake at this time. Begin new ventures that feed your spiritual path. Break away from old outworn ideas. If you are a man, find ways to embrace your inner woman. If you are a woman, find ways to embrace your inner man.

Positive affirmations are positive repetitive statements (said in the present tense). They act like a meditative mantra, and will break negative thought patterns that are no longer serving you. These may have been built up over the years and can actually begin to manifest as physical illnesses. Use the Equinox to look at areas of imbalance in yourself and use positive affirmations to help rebuild positive thought patterns for the future.

Decorate eggs, either hard-boiled or blown. Hard-boiled eggs can be rolled down a hill or eaten for breakfast. Special decorated eggs can be given as gifts to each other.

Plant seeds of herbs and native plants for medicine. Each bring a packet of seeds and a tray of compost. Share the seeds around so each will have a variety of useful plants.

There is a tradition of decorating hats with ribbons and spring flowers at the Spring Equinox (Easter bonnets).

Flying things

Make all kinds of things to fly in the wind. Using basket maker's willow, streamers of crepe paper, ribbons and wool, create shapes that you can run with in the wind.

1. Make a circle of willow and tie or tape on coloured streamers, the string at three points to balance at the centre, and then tie on a piece of string. It looks great flying along behind you as you run.

2. Sew together two circles of felt (about 7cm in diameter). Leave a small gap and fill with small brown lentils or rice. Sew in several long ribbons and then sew the whole thing up. This is great thrown up high into the air, streamers flying as it falls to Earth.

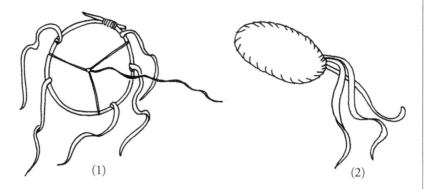

(1)   (2)

3. Make prayer flags or prayer sticks, writing your positive affirmations onto material and attaching them to sticks to stand in the wind. Send your prayers and messages out into the wind and out into the world. Fly dragon flags, dragon kites. Make dragon masks that can be attached to a long stick with streamers flying from the mask.

As part of theatre, plays or dance-theatre, have a dragon procession led by the dragon you have made. If this is done at night, everyone can carry candle lanterns and night lights in jars as part of a spectacular and memorable evening. Weave the path of the dragon's meandering path, activate and energise, dance and celebrate the return of the dragon or serpent energy.

Other plays and theatre can be performed in the round, exploring other Equinox themes of balance, birth and life awakening.

Dance to celebrate the first day of spring. Begin by imagining yourself curled up inside an egg or a seed. You are your egg or seed space. This is your world in the dark, growing life, incubating your plans, waiting. Feel the life force growing within you. Feel the new you who is waiting to be born into the light, into action, who will become manifest. As you begin to move outwards and break out of your shell or seed case, take with you your most positive intent, breathe new life into yourself as you break through into a new phase of your life. Celebrate and dance this power and energy. Celebrate being alive.

Bring the group back into a circle for the closing ceremony, holding hands and humming to attune and blend the energies which have been raised. If you are celebrating on your own, return to the still point at the centre of your being. Thank the energy of the Earth, the Air, Fire, Water, and Spirit. Thank the guardians and spirit guides. Thank the nature spirits and elementals, and thank each other.

Bless the food and drink to share.

THE KISS.

BELTAIN

SPRING CROSS QUARTER FESTIVAL

End April/Beginning May

MID-TAURUS ♉ FIXED EARTH

Full Moon

*Bel-tene * Walpurgisnact*
*Celtshaman * Bealtainn*
May Eve/May Day

Festival of Fertility
Festival of Expectation
Feast of Life

BELTAIN

Beltain is a celebration of the fertility and rampant potency of the life force. All of nature is growing and manifesting now in a wild whirl of creative energy. This is the time to celebrate unions of all kinds, fertility and manifestation on many different levels, love, sexuality and fruitfulness. It is a time to be in touch with the instinctive wild forces within and without, to be aware of the potency of the life force and its power on the physical, spiritual and mystical levels.

IN THE PAGAN PAST, this was the night of the 'greenwood marriage' where the union between the horned god and the fertile goddess was re-enacted by the men and the women to ensure the fertility of the land. It was a night to spend in the woods, to make love outside, stay up all night and watch the sunrise, and bathe in the early morning dew. On this night, people walked the mazes and labyrinths and sat all night by sacred wells and healing springs whose waters were said to be especially potent at this time. This was the 'merry month' when people dressed in green in honour of the Earth's new spring colours and the faerie folk, elementals and nature spirits, who are easier to meet at this time.

The horned god, Herne the Hunter, untameable instinctive wild man of the forest, becomes a white stag and chases the fertile goddess who becomes a white deer. The legend tells us he becomes the prey he hunts, and is magically transformed by his union with the goddess. Since prehistoric times there have been many images of horned gods: Actaeon the Stag, Pan the Goat, Dionysus or Zeus the Bull, Amen the Ram. There is a connection between horns and male vitality through an ancient tantric belief that by the transformation of ejaculation, a mystic energy mounts up the spine, made visible by horns, and brings mystical power and wisdom. A composite of all these horned gods of the Pagan religions became the Christian version of the devil. His lustful nature gives rise to the modern slang word 'horny', but the word lust in old German meant 'religious joy' and holds a clue to the transformation which takes place in the horned god as he releases his seed and brings fertility to the land.

The goddess is Epona, Rhiannon and Macha who rides her horse across the sky; and Grain, and Creiddylad, free and powerful spirits of womanhood, who knows the power of love and the power of her own sexuality. She too is transformed by their union, becoming the Grain-Mother, carrying the fruit of their union.

Together these gods and goddesses represent the great circle of life and death through the seasons. Through the blending of these opposite forces, they become the fertile force of manifest energy. Through their sacred union, they become transformed both physically and beyond the physical. Beltain is the celebration of this mystical and spiritual transformation inherent in sexual union.

May Day celebrations included dancing around the maypole, symbolising the interweaving and joining of the male and female energies. This creates a web of energy in a living matrix of power. It was common practice to bring a new pole into the village every year, representing the year's incarnation of the vegetation or nature spirit. Incorporated into the maypole dance was the green man who danced around the edge and represented the spirit of vegetation. All this is linked to a much older ceremony of fetching a living tree into the village every year (possibly a hawthorn tree). This living tree would still have its resident dryad within the tree who would be central to the ceremony and danced around. It would have been asked for its help to ensure fertility of the land and a good harvest. The popular song, "Here we go gathering nuts in May," probably refers to the 'knots' of May (Hawthorn) that were gathered for the Beltain celebrations. It is entirely the wrong month for nuts! These 'knots of May' were used to decorate houses, doorways and each other.

Another folklore custom of this time is the tying of ribbons and shreds of clothing to the hawthorn trees, especially where they grow by sacred wells. Dipped in the water, they are then hung in the trees with prayers for healing, and as gifts to the fair or faerie folk and the guardian spirits of the well or spring.

'Cast ne'er a clout before May is out' may not refer to the uncertainty of the weather (they have a similar expression in Northern Spain where the weather is very settled by this time), but may bear some reference to the woodland revelries, as it is no good wearing new clothes to go for a frolic in the woods. Old clothes can be torn and then hung in the Hawthorn trees!

Beltain is one of the four great Cross Quarter Fire festivals. A bel-tene means a goodly fire. A special fire was kindled after all the other fires in the community had been put out. This was the Tein-eigin, the Need Fire. People then jumped the fire to purify, cleanse, and to bring fertility. Couples jumped the fire together to pledge themselves to each other. At the end of the evening, the villagers would take some of the Tein-eigin to start their fires at home anew.

The church changed the focus of Beltain eve from a night of revelry and sexual potency, to the May Day celebration whose May queen was a symbol of virginity, purity and chastity. This transformed the wild sexually potent fertile goddess into her opposite and began the steady repression of sexual expression, especially the sexuality of women.

Beltain energy is one of reverence for all of life, celebrating and honouring the fertility that grows from the union of opposites. It is about the sacredness and power of unbridled love and sexual pleasure, and deep connections of the heart. Here at Beltain these powerful life forces are not just focused on sexual union, but unions of all kinds. Integrity of intention brings the physical and spiritual into balance. This creates a strong life force energy that releases the alchemy of manifestation. At Beltain, direct your focus to pledge your allegiance to the Earth, especially now when there are large areas of land all over the world dying from humankind's mismanagement, pollution, and intensive farming methods.

THE UNDERLYING
ENERGY OF BELTAIN

THIS IS THE BEGINNING of the final and most actively potent
of the waxing phases of the Sun's cycle. All of life is bursting
with fertility and the power of its own potential. Everything is
in the process of becoming. This is the peak of the spring season
and the beginning of summer, the onset of the growing season
when the Earth is clothed in green. Flowers are everywhere,
birds and animals are having their young, and the sounds of
birdsong fill the air. It is a time of sunshine and rain, swelling
and bursting, rising sap and fresh new growth. The Earth's
energies are at their most active. The dragon paths can be
intuitively sensed or dowsed. This is the perfect time for walking
these ancient energy paths.

Beltain, like its opposite on the wheel of the year, Samhain, marks
a particularly potent transition in the yearly cycle. At dawn and
dusk especially, the boundaries between the worlds are thin, and
we may find ourselves 'spellbound' by the power of the moment,
and experience the paranormal. This will bring insights and
understanding which will greatly expand our consciousness.

From here to Summer Solstice is the peak of the sunlight and
the conscious outward expression of ourselves. During this high-
energy time, we need to be aware of where we are and what we
want and need. Create the most fertile and positive environment
in which to grow the seeds of yourself. Reach out for what it is
that you want and let the energy of growth whisk you along.

This is a time to honour sex in its raw state, to see this as part of
the cycle, to allow the extreme to exist as part of nature and the
expansive energy.

Beltain brings the blending of opposites: the rational and the
intuitive, the active and the receptive, Fire and Water. Fertility is
inherent in everything, everything is possible. Manifestation is
reaching the height of its power.

Look at you – Father Sky
all puffed up proud and swollen
Clouds float dazzling
in sunshine and sapphire blue
piercing and penetrating...

Look at you – Mother Earth
so soft and wet, squelching and sucking
                              Juicy sap rising
in every lip and bud
swelling and bursting
into frothy flower and frond
How you glow in your new bright green!

Look at me, your child, a little animal
surrendered to the sweet sex of spring,
my pulse races with the urgent breath
rising and falling in the soft silk tummy
of the sleeping newborn lamb...

My heart sings fit to burst
and flies with the busy birds
flashing feathers flutter
as they lift into the blue...
and I'm buzzing with it all,
lazily meandering among bluebells and primroses
gulping down the sweetness,
poking my nose in moss, stone, bark, mud...

I walk, and a thousand blades of fresh new grass
vibrate
trembling diamond drops
catch rainbows from the sun
and my dreams of you and me
spiral up and up and up
– away we go –
a pair of buzzards soaring
with gliding outstretched wings.

Nicky Martin

PREPARATIONS FOR BELTAIN

Sacred Springs and Wells
Pilgrimage
Making Flower Essences
Making a Talisman
The Green Man * *Sheela-na-gig* * *Maypole*
Folk-dancing * *Wearing the Green*
Hand fasting * *Labyrinths*
Tree of Beltain: Hawthorn
Herbs of Beltain: Cowslip, Rosemary

Aim to celebrate Beltain on the night of the Full Moon, nearest to the end of April, and the beginning of May, or as near to this as possible. Plan to stay up all night, have a fire outside and enjoy being outside under the night sky. Watch the Sun come up and wash your face in the early morning dew. Dress in green to signify your allegiance to the Earth.

Springs and Wells

Visit springs and wells in your locality. If there are hawthorn trees growing nearby, sit and find stillness with these beautiful friendly trees. Hang ribbons in the trees in this age-old Beltain custom – to honour the tree, the nature spirits and to ask for healing. It is quite possible that this will inspire other people to do the same, and before long there will be many things hanging in the tree. Feel your heart and mind open with love for the Earth. Sing to the tree, meditate, and see what connections you make. Expand your consciousness and reach out to sense any spirits of the place, guardians or nature spirits. Follow your intuition. Keep an open mind.

Get out on the land to intuit and walk the dragon paths of activated Earth energies. You may wish to work with a pendulum or dowsing rods. Begin by focusing your intention to locate the dragon paths, and clearly establish which movement of the pendulum or rods represents 'yes'. You can also use either hazel or rowan twigs: Cut a new forked twig, grip each fork in each hand, pull them apart until you feel the pressure 'bite'. As the twig passes over underground water, it twists and twitches in the hand. If you sense any areas where the energy is stuck or congested, you may place crystals here or stake the Earth with a copper rod.

Pilgrimage

Make a pilgrimage or sacred journey, perhaps walking from one sacred spot to another. Tune into the energy of the Earth. Some ancient sites may contain the memories of previous times and may have guardians attached to them. Strange coincidences, phenomena of the natural world, seeing sudden images in rocks, trees and clouds, omens and impressions, should all be noted as significant when on a pilgrimage or sacred journey. Take food and drink with you, perhaps a wooden whistle, notebook or sketchbook, and make a day of it. The ancient sites still retain a power that can shift our perceptions outside of time.

Making Your Own Flower Essences

You will need a small glass bowl, a bottle of spring water, a small dark bottle, a little brandy, and a sunny day! Sit with the plant or tree first, admiring its beauty. Stand your glass bowl next to the plant or tree, gently adding a few flowers and leave in the sunshine. Intuit, write or draw and see what thoughts come to you. When you feel that the essence and spirit of the plant has entered the water, scoop off the flowers using a stalk or leaf from the same plant, and mix the water with equal parts of brandy to preserve it. This is the Mother Essence and should be treated with great respect. Pour into a dark jar and decorate a special label for it. Keep it close by you. After a few days, the Mother Essence can be made into a stock essence by adding seven drops to a 10ml bottle containing half brandy and half spring water. Keep the stock and the Mother Essence together for a few days. This makes a happier and more effective remedy. Take four drops from your stock bottle three times a day in a little water or straight on to the tongue, and note the subtle changes in your emotions, perceptions and life force energy that the plant can bring. These remedies will keep for years, ready to be used when needed.

Making a Talisman

A talisman holds beneficial or healing energy. To cut a piece of wood for this purpose, sit with a tree you are drawn towards and ask to be guided to a piece of wood you can cut. Thank the tree for its gift. As you whittle your talisman, focus on what you wish to use it for. Be clear in your intent. When you have finished carving, leave it to dry out before sanding it to a smooth finish using first a coarse, then a medium, and then fine sandpaper. Hang it round your neck or carry it in your pocket as a 'touch-wood'.

The Maypole

This is a pole with an equal number of alternate contrasting ribbons attached to the top. This can be embedded into a deep hole in the ground or fixed to a base. The dancers each have a ribbon and their interweaving dances produce a pattern of ribbons around the pole, representing the union of the male and the female. The pole can be dug into the ground or sunk into a base which is pegged down

Prepare a staff to take with you to the Beltain celebration. Either cut a new stick or decorate an old stick. Wrap bells and ribbons around it. Great to dance with, shake and brandish! Wrap small bells around your ankles and legs so that when you dance, you also make rhythm.

Sheela-na-gig

Also to be found hidden in the old churches are the Sheela-na-gigs, a carved naked woman squatting with knees apart, displaying her vulva. Her vulva is most often carved as a double-pointed oval, a common genital/yonic symbol known as the vesica piscis (the vessel of the fish). This fish symbol is found worldwide to represent female genitals, the Great Mother, the Creatress. Most Sheela-na-gigs have one or both hands drawing open the vulva. Many have deeply furrowed ribcages, perhaps linking their potent sexuality with death and the cyclic nature of fertility, life and death. Her open vulva is an invitation to her potent dark womb. Many have been destroyed, especially when Victorian prudery was at its height. Many were defaced or removed and have been found buried near the church. The ones that remain can be found hidden behind fonts, and in dark corners. In the past her vulva was touched for luck and many are worn smooth from much touching.

Handfasting

This is an old form of sacred marriage between two people, a ceremony, a pledge to last a year and a day and then be renewed every year. The couple write and say their own vows to each other. Usually a celebrant or friend will join their right hands together to unite their male souls and then join left hands to unite their female souls. This forms the figure of eight infinity sign with their arms crossed. The hands can then be loosely wrapped or bound in a special ribbon or scarf to signify their joining. The celebrant either follows their intuition for the binding or a Celtic knot pattern. Handfastings are usually held outside under the trees, under the sky. For some couples the hand fasting is all that they want to do and they renew their vows every year. For others it is a deeply potent addition to a more formal legally binding ceremony of marriage.

The Green Man
Throughout the Celtic lands are many images and stories of green men and green women. They represent the spirit of nature or the spirit of vegetation and they usually consist of the head only, surrounded in leaves, or sprouting leaves like horns, or pouring vegetation from their mouths, eyes, ears, horns. Old churches were built on the sites of Pagan worship and the early churches incorporated Pagan images to encourage the people to worship there. Many of the images displayed from the old religions contrived to be touched for luck and had offerings made to them, despite the church's desire to demonise them. Many green men look distinctly female or androgynous – a nature spirit being, neither male nor female, both aspects honoured. There are hundreds of these carved foliated heads hidden in our old churches, surviving from a time when the green man was of great significance and importance to the people of these lands. It is an interesting archetype to work with, either through visualisation or meditation. Honour this energy by making a green man out of willow whips. Weave them into a basic head framework and on Beltain eve, weave it with fresh greenery of all kinds pouring from its mouth and eyes. Use hawthorn for fertility and oak as a potent reference to the Sun king who reaches the height of his power between now and the Summer Solstice.

Labyrinths
Building a simple labyrinth is not as difficult as you might think. The first considerations are availability of materials and where to build it. It need not be enormous as long as it can be walked. Three metres across is enough for a small one, you may have room in your garden or on some land you may have access to. Stones can be used if you build it in a wild place where there are lots of stones lying around. For a more permanent site, it may be cut from the turf, or as gravel or mosaic paths. Hoops of hazel or willow can define it, with herbs along its pathways. Indoors its pattern may be laid down in free flowing cooking salt, or dry potting compost. Both can be swept up easily afterwards.

This is a very simple three-ringed labyrinth and is very quick to lay out.

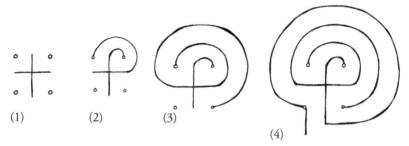

This is a classical seven-coil labyrinth. Larger and more complex (about 5m in diameter) but good for a permanent site, see below:

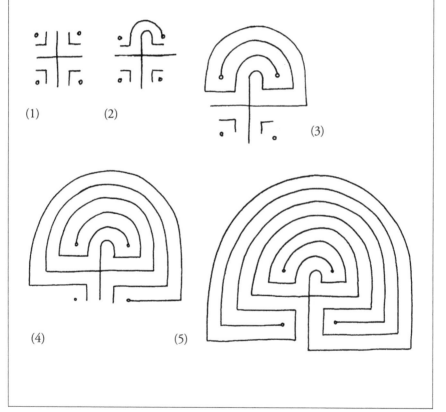

Try this unusual labyrinth that retains a continuous flow, while offering a choice of direction at the beginning.

See page 57 for more about labyrinths.

TREES OF BELTAIN

HAWTHORN – *Crataegus mongyna*

The May Tree, Whitethorn, Quickthorn, Haegthorn

This is the sixth Tree of the Celtic Tree Ogham: HUATH. H. and brings the spirit of wild places with it, even when growing in a town. Said to be the haunt of faeries, and

love and fertility. Later, as the Christian religion took hold, these were reversed and it was said to be an unlucky tree, representing chastity, sexual abstinence and misfortune. But once again it is seen as a positive symbol of the heart. It is particularly potent for healing affairs of the heart and can be given as a token of friendship and love. It will help release blocked energy, release stress and fears, and open the flow for healing and open-hearted loving communication.

The flowers, leaves, and particularly the berries, are prized as a cardiac tonic that acts in a normalizing way upon the heart by either stimulating or depressing its activity, depending on the need. It may be used safely for long periods of time, for heart weakness, palpitations, high blood pressure and angina.

Use to strengthen the body in old age by drinking an infusion of the berries daily. Also in times of stress. Pour one cup of boiling water onto two teaspoons of the dried berries. Leave covered for twenty minutes. Drink three times a day for long periods. Alternatively cover with cold water and leave overnight.

In the spring, drink the blossom as a tea for a spring tonic that helps the heart and circulation. If you want to collect and dry the flowers yourself, pick them on a dry sunny morning and hang them to dry in brown paper bags in a warm airy place. When they are completely dry, seal them in a dark, airtight container or jar. Gather them fresh every year. Use the fresh flowers in salads and fruit salads. Eat the young leaf shoots straight from the tree (known as bread and cheese) or toss those into salads too.

HERBS OF BELTAIN

COWSLIP – *Primula veris*

On May morning, posies of cowslips would be given as a token of friendship and love. Associated with the Norse goddess Freya and the Roman goddess Venus, both linked to love and sexuality. It used to grow freely everywhere, but in the UK is now a protected plant, so grow it yourself from native seed and then re-introduce it into the wild. It is a safe herb to use with babies, children and the elderly. Use for mild insomnia and headaches, and as a general nerve tonic. It is also beneficial to the lungs and can be used at night to calm a dry irritating cough. It will help clear the body of poisons. Make an infusion using a handful of fresh flowers to 600ml of boiling water. Cover and leave for ten minutes. Strain and keep in the fridge. Drink one wineglassful three times a day. Drink when you want to lift the spirits.

ROSEMARY – *Rosmarinus officinalis*

Ruled by the Sun, rosemary has a vibrant stimulating energy. It is a symbol of fertility and used in marriage and hand fasting ceremonies. It can be burnt as incense and has an uplifting energy. Pick some fresh sprigs of rosemary, pour on boiling water, cover and leave for ten minutes. Strain off the herb and drink a wineglassful three times a day. This same liquid can be used as an antiseptic on wounds, for bites and stings. To ease muscular pains and neuralgia pour a mixture into the bath. It is a stimulant for the whole system and will strengthen the heart and increase circulation. Use whenever the body is sluggish and the limbs are cold. It will raise low blood pressure. It will lift the spirits; chase away lethargy, anger, hatred, grief and bitterness. It increases blood flow to the head and can be used as a mental stimulant instead of caffeine. It will improve memory and aid concentration.

Warning! Do not use rosemary if there is a history of high blood pressure or if you are pregnant.

BELTAIN CELEBRATIONS

These are some suggestions for celebrating Beltain.

Beltain is best celebrated outside, where you can have a fire and the freedom to drum and be exuberant!

The fire is central to Beltain eve. Ask everyone to bring special logs and dried herbs for the fire. Build the fire beforehand so that within whatever ceremony you devise, the fire can be lit with impact and certainty. Carefully make the sacred fire using known wood from native trees. This is the Bel-tene, the good fire, bringing healing purifying energies and fertility, and should be lit with invocation and blessings.

Make a beautiful shrine area with spring flowers and greenery. Light a candle for each element and represent each of them here. Represent the horned god and the green goddess in some way, either with figures of clay or bone, or by suggestion, using materials such as antlers, horn or tree branches.

Wear green in honour of the Earth and her new colour.

Each make a headdress of greenery by weaving a circle of willow or other flexible plant, to fit the head and then wrapping other greenery around it. (See page 50.) Weave the power of your new direction as you work. Sing a chant that enhances this energy.

Have a masked ceremony with everyone wearing greenery masks. Masks that only cover the top half of the face are the most practical as they leave the mouth free to speak, eat and drink. (See pages 47-49.)

Ask everyone to bring food and drink to share, and after the ceremony, have a great feast.

Make the most use of drumbeat and other music. Dancing will energise, relax and release energy. It is a good way to begin a ceremony as it brings the group together. Let a peak be reached and then bring the energy down again, and gather the group into a circle.

Honour each of the Five Elements in turn. Face their direction and all speak from the heart to raise awareness and celebrate their gifts.

Air in the East
We thank the element of Air and our breath, which gives us life. Through our voices we celebrate the Earth, the springtime season. We celebrate our power to communicate. We ask that our thoughts and words are focused and inspired. Our words have power. Invocation has power. May we use our words wisely. We give thanks for the power of song and music.

Fire in the South
We thank the Sun for warming the Earth, for bringing new growth and abundance. We thank Fire for the creative spark. What do we initiate at this time? We thank Fire for our passion, for self-expression and our sexuality. The active power of Fire brings us the energy to transform and change our lives. The power of our 'Yes!' can change the world! We give thanks for our freedom; for the gift of spontaneity; for our ability to make things happen; for all that we create and manifest.

Water in the West
We give thanks for Water that gives us life, for the rain that brings growth and fertility. We give thanks for our love that helps us to follow our hearts most positive and loving intent. We give thanks for our intuition that brings guidance from within. We welcome our receptivity to these subtle energies deep within ourselves and within the natural world. May we learn how to share and learn from our emotions and deepest feelings and how to grow with loving kindness and compassion.

Earth in the North
We send our Love and thanks to the Earth for all its gifts, and the power of the life force and all that is being made fertile. We celebrate all the beauty, all the new growth of the flowers and of the trees, and all the new born creatures and birds. We give thanks for the great abundance of the natural world and all that we manifest in our lives right now. We give thanks to the Earth for the new seeds that are growing strong and bless the young crops that will become our food.

Spirit at the Centre

We give thanks for our ever-deepening connection to our spiritual path. We reach out to experience the source of life and listen to guidance from our inner knowing and integrity. We welcome and thank all our guardian angels and spirit guides and are open to trust in the power of our unconditional love and the wisdom of our hearts.

The words I have written here are intended as clues and pathways to understanding. When invoking the elements, it is important to speak from the heart and with power, so that you help to make the connection strong for yourself and all those present. Use the elemental charts on pages 30-34 to help you.

Use the mesmerising effect of Fire, candles and drumbeat to evoke a trance-like atmosphere. Altered states of consciousness bring deep insights and help us slip between the worlds and into a timeless state. Honour what comes up for you in these moments and share your insights with each other.

Explore ways to connect to the wild man and wild woman energy. Openly express this wild energy through dress, dance, voice and celebrate your sexuality.

Pass around a sacred marriage basket. Let each person use it as a focus for their hopes, gifts and blessings for their relationships.

Focus on the heart chakra that is green, the colour of life and love, and the throat chakra that is blue, the colour of communication. The energy between the heart and the voice brings communication from the heart (turquoise). Use this fertile time to walk your talk, and to express yourself from your inner truth. Use this potent time between now and the Summer Solstice to say what you want to say, and to focus your direction. Pass round a piece of turquoise stone and let each person speak from the heart.

Create a temporary labyrinth (see pages 134 and 136). Walk this ancient pathway in a walking meditation, seeking clarity, being open to receive inspired thoughts. Write any insights down afterwards.

Whistling women were believed to conjure up destructive storms. Therefore, during the centuries of witch-hunts, girls and women were not allowed to whistle. It is used in sympathetic magic to raise a wind, and to draw in and send out energy. Explore your abilities to use whistling in this way or use as a focus for sending healing. Focus a low whistle first, making it resonate with the base chakra. Move on up the chakras finding the note/s that resonate for each one. Explore where your resonance lies and any changes that occur as a result.

Learn to whistle the calls of birds. There are many possibilities here for exploring these channels of shamanic communication.

Look at what you are currently manifesting. Will it lead to the harvest you wish for? If it does, then find further ways to help the flow of this energy; if it doesn't, then now is the time to plant new seeds and nurture them so that they can grow strong and well. Envision what it is you want. Believe you deserve it and that it has already begun. This is the alchemy of positive manifestation and prosperity consciousness. Envision it as established already.

If it is a clear night, find Venus, the wishing star, and make a wish as you align yourself to her.

To dance a maypole dance successfully, you really need to find someone to teach you and a folk band to play the tunes (a simple 'scratch' band is enough). A few practices beforehand really helps too as even the simplest of dances can result in the ribbons getting tangled. The interweaving of the two colours of ribbon form a pattern down the length of the pole that is undone as the direction of the dance is reversed.

Folk Dances

A simple interweaving circle dance without a maypole can be fun to do and it doesn't matter so much if you get mixed up. Begin by making a circle of equal pairs who face each other. Decide who is 'A' or 'B'. All of the 'A's face one way and all of the 'B's face the other way. Taking right hands, pass on the right shoulder and reach for the next person's left hand. Pass on the left shoulder and reach for the next person's right hand, and so on. This pattern of interweaving can be continued until the couples reach their starting partner and they can then dance together, spinning off to dance with others as well.

Another simple dance ritual, known as the wolf-dance, consists of men and women separating and making a line on opposite sides of a room or dance area. To the rhythm of drums or other instruments, they then advance towards each other dancing, slinking, swirling, making eye contact, until they pass each other. At this point they reach out to grab someone and twirl around together before moving back into their line. This can be repeated many times. Great fun!

Create your own dance rituals that reflect unions, courtship, the chase, and the blending of energies that signify Beltain. Have someone dressed up as the green man to lead the ritual dance or to interact with a chaotic wild energy.

Many folk dances can be learnt with the help of a good caller and a barn dance band. Learn the simple dances that enable you to forget about watching and counting, and allow you to slip into the pattern of movement that is the inner ritual of the dance.

Dance around a favourite tree or use a tree in a pot placed in the centre of the circle. Light candles to honour the tree kingdom and the dryads. Thank them for their help to humankind. Be careful not to singe the tree with the candle flame. Alternatively make a circle around a tree you are drawn towards. Link to the tree's energy, hug the tree and feel its presence and powerful life force. Tone long slow notes with the tree for at least ten minutes or more while you align your self with the essential spirit of the tree.

Jumping the Beltain fire is an age-old Beltain tradition. Jump and say what you leave behind in the fire! Jump and call out what you fire up and energise in your life right now! Jump as a couple and pledge yourselves to each other! Jump as friends and fire up plans you will do together this year!

Come together in a circle for the closing ceremony. Hold hands and feel your connection to each other, and the love and the friendship that celebrating together has brought. If you are celebrating on your own, return to the centre of your being and focus on all that you love in your life right now. Thank the elements for their gifts, thank the nature spirits, the guardians and the spirit helpers for their presence, and thank each other. End on a chant to energise and enhance the power of Beltain.

Bless the food and drink that everyone brought to share. Have a feast and party!

SUMMER SOLSTICE

SUMMER QUARTER POINT
20th-23rd June

SUN ENTERS CANCER ♋

The longest day and shortest night

Midsummer's Eve
Midsummer's Day
*Litha * St John's Day*

Festival of Attainment

Celebration of the Return of the Dark

SUMMER SOLSTICE

The Sun enters the sign of Cancer ♋ as her rays shine down on Earth directly at the furthest point North in the annual cycle (the Tropic of Cancer). In the Northern Hemisphere it is the longest day (24 hours of sunshine North of the Arctic circle). The Sun is at the height of its power, but now is the second great turning point in the solar year, where the cosmic wheel stops and starts again. This is the longest day, but from now on the days will shorten.

ON MIDSUMMER'S EVE PEOPLE stayed up all night to watch the sunrise and celebrate the longest day. Bonfires of oak wood were lit on the hilltops and aromatic herbs thrown into them. Cattle and the sick were passed through the smoke for healing and good health. People leaped the fires to rid themselves of misfortune and to assure abundance in love and the fertility of the land. The wheel is an important symbol of this festival but unlike at the Winter Solstice, when all wheels were stopped, here wheels are kept in motion. Cartwheels swathed in straw were lit and rolled down the hillsides. They were called fate wheels and the abundance of the harvest depended on how well and how far these blazed.

Midsummer's eve was a night of candlelit and torch lit processions, which usually took a circular route, known as a carousel, or wheel of chariots. This is the origin of the carnival procession celebrating the great cosmic wheel of the year, 'She Who Turns the Year', the 'Goddess of the Wheel', Fortuna, the Wheel of Fate, Lady Luck, Dame Fortune. It was a time of dancing and joyful abandonment, a celebration of the 'Corn Mother-Goddess', Ceridwen, Cerealia, Ceres, Demeter. Giant effigies of the Earth Mother, green men and dragons were carried through the town and later burnt on the Midsummer fires. Farmers would circle their crops three times with lighted torches in celebration of the Earth Mother and the harvest that was to come. Ships were wheeled through the towns and villages (the origins of the carnival float). Both the ship and the ark were symbols of the womb of the Earth, the germ of life, and the dark inner world beginning now. With the new cycle of the Sun begins the journey to the Summerlands, signifying endings and beginnings. The outer energy begins to wane. The inner energy begins to expand.

This is a dual celebration. On the one hand, it is a celebration of all which has become manifest during the outward cycle of the Sun, and on the other hand, it celebrates the return to the dark cycle of the year. Sometimes two fires were lit to express this duality. From now on the cycle begins to change and a magical transformation begins. At this point of fulfilment and power, the Sun becomes one with the swelling of the grain and the new seed within, the joining of the active and receptive principles. This was symbolised by the sacred marriage of Jupiter and Juno (Roman) and Zeus and Hera (Greek). It was an important occasion in the old calendar, and many stone circles are aligned to the Solstice sunrise so that this peak of the solar year could be acknowledged.

But more than this, it is an acknowledgment of the coming return of the dark. Here we are called upon to value the power of the dark cycle as a necessary part of the whole, to celebrate its rich potency, its nurturing and receptive nature, and see it as a gift, vital to us all and to the Earth. Amidst the revelries of high summer, take a moment to acknowledge the equilibrium and balance this brings, and celebrate this too.

COME OUT DANCING

Get on your glad rags, sniff out the clues
It's a warm summer night for blue suede shoes
Someone, somewhere is playing the blues
So tune in, turn on, step out and

Come out dancing
Free the spirit
Find the laugh in your heart and beam it out

Come out dancing
Find the energy
Loosen limbs and limber up

Come out dancing
Defy gravity
Scatter inertia to the four winds

Come out dancing
Like a wild one
Dancing
Like a wild one
Dance like a wild one
Write your name in the sky

Brian Boothby
Tomorrows Ancestor

THE UNDERLYING ENERGY OF SUMMER SOLSTICE

Throughout all of nature the rampant growth period of the year has reached its peak and the natural world is in total manifestation. The trees are in full leaf and blossom, herbs, flowers and vegetables are flourishing and the fruit and grain are beginning to swell. Everywhere there is a sense of completeness and abundance.

The Summer Solstice is the peak of our expressive and expansive selves. It is known as the Festival of Attainment and celebrates the fulfilment of the individual. It is a time to enjoy and celebrate what you have, what and who you are, and what you have achieved and manifested this year. Use this special day to focus and charge with healing and positive intent all you wish to be. Add the strength and power of the Sun to enhance and activate what you want to bring into your life. Abandon yourself to expressive dance, song, joy and a sense of your own uniqueness.

Here at the peak of this active solar energy, a transformation and alchemy is taking place. The active principle now fires up the inner journey, bringing spiritual rebirth and completion of our whole selves. Celebrate the death and rebirth of the great cycle of the year. As the power of the outer realms wane, the power of the inner realms will expand, and we are made whole.

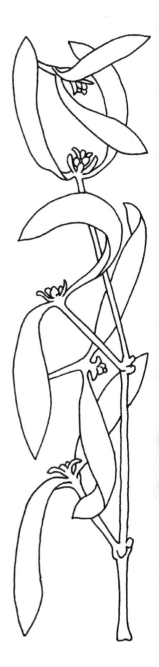

PREPARATIONS FOR SUMMER SOLSTICE

*Collecting and Drying Herbs * Herb Pillow*
*Herb Sachets * Medicine Bags or Shaman's Pouch*
*Creating a Wheel of Power * Sweat Lodge*
*The Rose * Mistletoe*
*Trees: Holly * Oak*
*Herbs: Elderflower * Lavender*
*Lemon Balm * St John's Wort*

Summer Solstice, like Winter Solstice, is a time for gathering together with like-minded people. Many people go to the stone circles on Midsummer's eve to stay up all night and watch the Solstice sunrise. This is an opportunity to meet and be with fellow kindred spirits. If you are organising a Midsummer celebration, find somewhere to be outside where you can have a fire, make music and dance, where there is enough outdoor space for a procession and for camping out. Ask everyone to bring firewood, as well as food and drink for a feast.

Because it is the longest day, it will not get dark until late. If the Moon is full and the night clear, it will not really get dark at all, but if the Moon is new, you will need some candle lanterns and night-lights in jars for those few hours between dark and dawn.

A procession can be as elaborate as you have the time and energy to make it. Traditionally wicker dragons and Earth Mothers were carried or wheeled along in a cart. Making large effigies for procession may take weeks of preparation, but will create a memorable occasion for all. Create the shapes you wish to make using basket maker's willow, weaving and binding over the joins with masking tape. When you are happy with the shape, soak strips of cotton sheet or paper in watered-down PVA glue and lay the strips over the wicker base. Later more material can be glued over the top of this base and painted with acrylics when dry. Coloured and shiny materials can be glued on top of the finished painted structure for added effect.

Create an area where you will have the feast, with tables to put the food on and places to sit. Decorated gazebos are always a good idea. Make streamers of organza, bunting to hang from trees, ribbons to fly in the wind. Find a way to hang up lanterns. Forked sticks cut from the hazel and pushed into holes in the ground are effective. Add vases of flowers and herbs in pots. All this helps to make a beautiful area, where people can relax and chat. It is a good idea to create place where children can get into sleeping bags safe and secure, with parents nearby. Ask everyone to bring rugs to put down for this purpose.

Create a space here for theatre and sacred drama to be performed in the round. Explore themes of transformation and changing cycles, the light and the dark. Masks for the play or procession will need to be made beforehand. Use lots of gold paint and any shiny gold material that will catch the light of the fire and candles. Encourage the children to perform.

Make a shrine to the Sun, preferably on a circular surface. Paint a Sun on a piece of cloth or board, or make an appliqué Sun cloth. These become lasting treasures that can be brought out and used whenever the Sun's energy needs to be invoked. Alternatively, gather gold, orange and red scarves and any sparkly gold materials to create a shrine to celebrate the power of the Sun and the Summer Solstice. Fill it with colour and light.

Solar Charged Elixirs

Place a glass of spring water in the Sun and after a few hours, drink the solar-charged water. You can add specific herbs and gemstones to the water to bring their unique properties to the solar-charged elixir. Wash all your crystals and stones and leave them to dry and charge in the Midsummer Sun.

Harvesting and Using Herbs

There are many herbs that are ready to be picked at this time and dried for winter cooking, teas, and medicines. Leaves are at the peak of their potency just before the flowers open, and flowers are at their peak of potency just as they are opening. Do not over-pick and thank the plants as you pick them. It is best to collect herbs into a basket or paper bags on a sunny day, when the dew has dried. If possible, pick aerial parts of the plant as the Moon is waxing to full. Choose only the best quality plants growing in big clumps away from roads or sprayed cultivated land. Use secateurs or scissors and do as little damage as possible. Hang up the herbs as quickly as possible, away from direct sunlight, in a dry airy place, or lay them out on clean sheets of paper, covering them with more paper and turning them frequently. You can also place the flower heads or leaves in brown paper bags and hang these up or place on sunny window ledges. Shake them and turn the flowers and leaves over frequently as they dry.

When they are fully dry, the leaves and flowers will crumble. Discard the stems. Store the dried herbs in brown paper bags or dark jars, as it is sunlight that reduces their properties. Keep them away from damp and label them at the time. Dried herbs should smell and taste as good as the fresh herbs. Leaves and flowers should be replaced every year.

The dried herb is twice as potent as the fresh herb, so if you wish to use the fresh herb, you need twice as much. The proportions do not need to be exact. A single dose can be made with one teaspoonful of the dried herb or a handful of the fresh. For the very young or the very old, make a weaker solution. For applying externally, make a stronger solution. To make a herbal infusion or tisane, pour boiling water over the herb and cover to keep in the essential oils. Leave to stand for ten minutes, then strain. The herbal liquid is usually drunk by the wineglassful three times a day. Some prefer it hot, sweetened with honey, (you can re-heat the liquid, but do not boil). Some prefer it cold, straight from the fridge. Alternatively, pour your wineglassful in a mug and top up with hot water.

N.B. Herbs need to be taken regularly over a period of time, but generally do not use any herb for more than twelve weeks because of the danger of certain chemicals building up in the body. Most minor conditions will improve within a few days, chronic problems within several weeks. As soon as the condition shows signs of improvement, gradually reduce the amount of herb until you feel you no longer need the remedy. Professional advice should be sought if there is no improvement after eight to twelve weeks, or if there is deterioration in the condition.

Medicine Bag, Crane Bag or Shaman's Pouch

Medicine and charm bags are small and contain herbs, charms or crystals used for healing. They are hung round the neck and worn next to the skin. The crane bag or shaman's pouch is much larger and is hung from the belt. The shaman's pouch is a record of your spiritual journey and each thing you place in it has significance, power and meaning to you, and will serve to remind you of an insight or healing gained. It might include wood from significant trees, tree and plant roots, and other natural finds. Shaman believe that some items contain spirit helpers and draw you to be attracted to them and pick them up, such as stones, shells, bone, crystals, feathers. If you later decide that they are no longer potent to you, return them to where the came from, or leave them in a special place, laying them back on or in the Earth with honour and thanks.

The best material to use is soft leather. Pieces of chamois leather are easy to obtain from car accessory shops. Vegans can use a fine woollen scarf, felt or calico. The size of your bag will depend on its use. Experiment with a piece of old material or paper napkin. Generally the diameter of a medicine bag will be approximately 8-10cm and a shaman's pouch will be 25-30cm.

1. Draw a circle using a compass or cup or plate of approximately the right size. Make holes in the leather all the way round about 1cm in from the edge and about 1cm apart. To make the holes, fold the leather and snip across the fold.

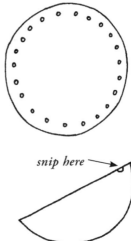

snip here

2. Either thread one long thong or two shorter thongs (40cm each for a shaman's pouch) through opposite directions, completing the circle at opposite sides. Experiment with a piece of string before cutting leather strips or buying leather thong. Use a bead as a fastening.

Making a Herb Pillow
Herb pillows need to be about 10-20cms rectangles and flat. They slip in the pillowcase and help a person sleep. Sew a material rectangle, turn it inside out, fill with dried herbs but keep flat. Re-sew around the outside edge with small running stitches to keep the herbs evenly distributed. Use lavender, hops, and lemon balm.

Making Herbal Bath Bags
Herbs can be absorbed through the skin as well as drunk. Cut a circle of fine muslin, place the dried herbs in the centre and gather the edges up to form a sachet. Tie embroidery thread or thin ribbon around the top. Place one or two sachets in a jug. Pour on boiling water. Cover and leave for ten minutes. Pour the solution into the bath. Use lavender for a relaxing bath or rosemary to energise you and help you to be mentally alert.

Wheel of Power
Create a permanent Wheel of the Year on the land to fix the eight points of the year. Stones or poles can be embedded in the Earth with due ceremony and ritual. Begin with a central pole or stone and establish its still point of power. Then, using a compass, turn it until the red arrow is on North. This establishes North and the directions and from this each of the quarter points: the Winter and Summer Solstices, North to South, and the Spring and Autumn Equinoxes, East to West. This also establishes the five elements with Spirit at the centre and around the circumference. The Cross Quarter Points, the four great Fire festivals of Imbolc, Beltain, Lammas and Samhain are the diagonal point in between. You now have a framework for working with and understanding the patterns and cosmology of the cycle of the year.

Many other systems can be woven into your wheel. Around the circle you might put the thirteen stones for each of the Moons of the year. The Tree Ogham, the Runes, planets and totem animals may also be represented. It will mean many things to you on many different levels as you work with it over the years. It becomes a place where the passage of time and your understanding of the underlying energy of its passing can be reviewed and experienced. At the centre is the still point where time stops. Here you can meditate and orient yourself to face the directions. It need not be a large circle and could easily be made in a garden, or as a small circle of stones out on the moors as a place to return to.

If it is not possible to make a permanent sacred wheel, then collect nine special stones or special pieces of wood or sticks, and make a temporary circle in a room or outside somewhere where you feel comfortable and relaxed. Place the first stone or stick in the centre and focus the still point of Spirit. Then, using a compass, place a stone on each of the Quarter Points, focussing on what you understand each to represent.

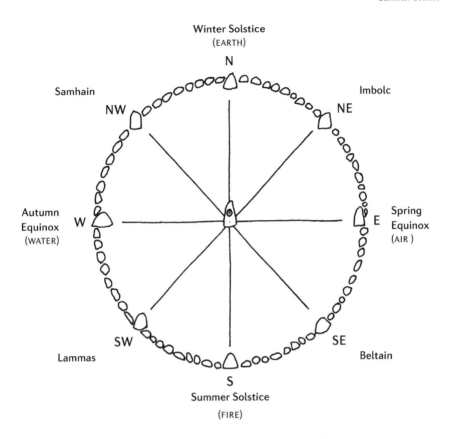

Winter Solstice
(EARTH)
N

Samhain

Imbolc

NW

NE

Autumn
Equinox
(WATER)

W

E

Spring
Equinox
(AIR)

SW

SE

Lammas

Beltain

S

Summer Solstice
(FIRE)

Finally place the stones or sticks for each of the four great Fire festivals, considering what they mean and how their passing is affecting you. Working in this way helps to understand the underlying energy and patterns of the solar year, the passage of time and our own journey within it.

Sweat Lodge

The sweat lodge is a shamanic tradition that has survived from many tribal cultures around the world and is an aid to physical and spiritual cleansing. It is now popular with those who celebrate the passing of the solar year, or the passage of the Moon. It is usually held at Full Moon or New Moon or at each of the Celtic festivals and is a ceremonial and sacred occasion. Volcanic stones (Basalt) are heated in a special fire. (It is important to get the right stones or they will explode in the fire and this can be very dangerous.) The fire is lit with due ceremony and once it has been built up with logs, the rocks are placed on top of the fire. Once the fire has died down, some of the stones are carried on a shovel into a pit inside the sweat lodge and water is gently poured onto the hot rocks to make steam. There are many traditions for doing this. It is always a sacred ritual. The simplest is to go in and out five times, dowsing yourself in cold water each time you come out, and bringing fresh hot stones in each time. Each time of entering the sweat lodge, a new element and direction is honoured and your truth within that element is shared with each other. There is often one person who will keep the focus of the ritual. The fifth and final time is a space for meditation and inner journeying. At the end when everyone has come out, the last hot stones are put in, water is poured on for the ancestors, and the door is closed.

The Rose
The Rose had special significance at this time and was used to decorate the sacred groves and the Midsummer's eve dancers. The wild rose or dog rose (*Rosa canina*)

How to Build a Sweat Lodge
This shows the framework of hazel rods with the pit in the centre for the hot stones. (Everyone sits around the edge.) The whole thing is covered with old blankets to make a good thick covering. Secure the blankets with rope thrown over the top and with stones around the bottom. A piece of canvas can be thrown over the top of the blankets for added strength and insulation, but it is not essential. A blanket is hung over the doorway.

You will need:
- 12-16 fresh hazel rods, approximately 3-4m long. The rod diameter should be about 3cms at the thick end
- A metal spike and a lump hammer
- Garden string
- Old blankets, rope, canvas, stones for weighing down the edges
- About 25 volcanic rocks (Basalt) that will not explode in the fire.

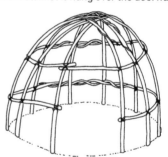

1. Decide on the size of the floor circle. About 4.5-5.5m diameter is a good size. Pair up the rods, choosing the thickest rods for the main structure. Make a 15cm hole with the metal spike and lump hammer, angled slightly outwards, and put in the first rod, thick end down. Then make the hole for the second rod opposite the first rod in the same way.

has five petals and was a symbol of The Goddess, Venus, Aphrodite, motherhood, regeneration and eternal life. It was used in ancient writing and poetry as a symbol of sexuality. Its five petals symbolise the five-pointed pentacle, a symbol of power and protection used since earliest times. The red rose signified mature or maternal sexuality while the white rose belonged to the virgin. The rose garden, the rose bush, the rose garland, and the rose wreath were all part of this symbolism of sexuality and the goddess. The chant 'ring around the rose wreath' referred to a traditional summer's dance known as the Rose, which was so popular, the church found it hard to suppress it. It has been said that a pocket full of posies referred to the cave of flowers, a symbol of a woman's sexuality, and 'all fall down' referred to the end of the fertile season. Five dancers with swords formed a five-pointed star over a victim called the Fool who was symbolically slain and resurrected with an elixir called the dewdrop of the rose. The dance held within it a key to the rites of Midsummer.

2. Bring the thin ends of hazel together to form an arch the height you wish your sweat lodge to be. Bend the ends round each other and tie with string to make them strong.

3. Continue making the archways opposite each other using the strongest rods, and tie them securely at the centre. Three pairs of rods are enough for a small sweat lodge. More pairs are needed for a bigger structure.

4. Use thinner rods for horizontal weaving. Wedge the thick end in, and use the thin end of the rod for the weaving around the upright rods to make it strong. Tie over where they join. Leave a door space.

5. In the centre, dig a pit for the hot stones, leaving enough space around for people to sit. Cover the whole thing with old blankets, with a blanket for the door. Weigh them down at the edges with stones. The whole structure can then be covered with a piece of canvas and ropes to hold it down. Reed or marsh grass can be strewn over the floor; or use coconut matting, old canvas, old carpet; or simply sit on the earth (although it can get very slippery and muddy as the sweat pours off you!).

6. Make a separate area with a hose, a cold shower or watering cans filled with water. Rebuild the fire after the first stones have been taken out so that each time of re-entering the sweat lodge, there are fresh hot stones. At the end, rebuild the fire so that everyone can come together around the fire to relax, eat, drink and socialise. It is good if someone is willing to take on the role of staying outside, heating the stones, building up the fire, refilling watering cans, organising the food and hot drinks.

TREES OF THE SUMMER SOLSTICE

OAK – *Quercus robur*

The oak tree is sacred to Druids and represents the doorway into the second half of the year at the Summer Solstice. It is the seventh tree in the Celtic Tree Ogham. DUIR. D. Its Celtic name '*Duir*' means doorway. The oak is dedicated to the Gods of Thunder: Zeus (Greek), Jupiter (Roman), Thor (Norse) – regarded as the great fertilising powers who sent rain and caused the Earth to bear fruit. The druids made distilled water from the flower buds to cleanse the internal body. Water found in the hollows of the tree was used ritually to cleanse the external body in readiness for the Summer Solstice. The oak is the Sun king whose attributes are strength, courage, inner peace, and the endurance to survive. Sit with the oak when you need to find the strength to face difficulties and sort out complicated problems. It will bring deep calm and restore self-determination. It creates a doorway to your inner spirituality and the power of love within.

MISTLETOE – *Viscus quercus*

Mistletoe was traditionally gathered on Midsummer's eve or Midsummer's day. To the Druids it was particularly potent when it grew on the oak. It was thought to be a very magical plant as it doesn't have its roots in the Earth, but appears high in the trees and has a life force of its own, perhaps sent as a gift from the gods. Wands of mistletoe wood were gathered at Midsummer when the mistletoe, like the Sun, was at the height of its power. These wands were placed under the pillow to induce dreams and omens.

HOLLY – *Ilex aquifolium*

This is the eighth tree of the Celtic Tree Ogham: TINNE. T. In the old legends the Oak King and the Holly King do battle at Midsummer and Midwinter. Holly is ruled by Mars, a fiery energy that brings movement and action. The holly tree represents everlasting life, recovery and restored direction. It helps us to find the raw energy needed to move beyond negative emotional reactions to bring unconditional love, clarity and understanding into our lives and all our actions. Holly is a tree of protection and was planted near to the house or hung over the door for this purpose. It helps guard against poisoned thoughts and bad vibrations.

HERBS OF THE SUMMER SOLSTICE

So many herbs are reaching their peak at this time of the year. Enjoy them now while they are fresh, and dry them for use during the rest of the year.

ELDERFLOWER – *Sambucus nigra*

The flowers make an excellent daily tonic tea. Place a handful of flowers in a jug and pour on boiling water. Cover and leave for ten minutes and drink sweetened with a little honey. This same infusion can be used as a skin tonic and a lotion for wounds, burns and rashes. Drink as a sedative to promote a peaceful sleep, for any catarrhal inflammations, coughs, sinusitis and hay fever. Useful for moving stuck emotionally congested states.

Make elderflower cordial for a wonderful Summer Solstice drink that is quick and easy to make. Put ten large flower heads in a large bowl with 600g of sugar, two chopped lemons, and 25g of tartaric acid. Pour on about 2.2lts of boiling water and stir well. Cover with a clean tea towel and leave for 24 hours, stirring occasionally. Strain through muslin or a tea towel, and bottle. It will keep for a week or freeze it in plastic bottles (do not overfill) for later use. Dilute with still or carbonated water.

LAVENDER – *Lavendula officinalis*

Lavender is a herb of the solar plexus, the area above the navel through which we assimilate and receive external stimuli. Some people pick up all kinds of vibrations and can be at the mercy of other people's emotions and feelings. Drinking lavender tea regularly will help to strengthen the inner discriminating faculties, so that equilibrium and peace are restored. Lavender is most useful in relieving stress and for all states of nervous debility, exhaustion, insomnia, physical and mental tension, and for migraines and headaches caused by stress or too much Sun. It will clear the blood of toxins, strengthen the liver, and will lower blood pressure. Make an infusion in the usual way. Pour a solution into your bath at the end of a hard day's work to relieve aching limbs and exhaustion. Burn it as an incense to bring clarity, visions for focusing the mind, and trance work.

LEMON BALM – *Melissa officinalis*

Make an infusion in the usual way and use as a tonic for the circulatory system and the heart, helping to lower blood pressure. It is also a good digestive tonic, helping to assimilate fatty foods. It is a useful herb for the menopause, helping to ease hot flushes, depression, anxiety and palpitations. It will also ease period pains and help regulate menstruation. It is safe to use in pregnancy for headaches, dizziness and morning sickness. Useful for colds and flu, it lowers fevers and promotes sweating. Rub the leaves directly onto insect bites. Lemon balm drives away all troubles and cares, lifts the spirits and eases depression. It is soothing, expansive, and opens the heart to giving and receiving love.

ST JOHN'S WORT – *Hypericum perforatum*

A herb of Midsummer. Pick at midday on a sunny day. The entire plant above ground is a valuable pain reducing anti-inflammatory and general healing remedy. Make the infusion in the usual way and use internally and externally for wounds, ulcers, blisters, burns, rashes, bruises and sunburn. It will clear congestion from the lungs, is good for irritating coughs, for any nerve pains such as neuralgia, and for menopausal changes of anxiety or irritability. An excellent massage oil can be made to help relieve tension, sciatica and rheumatic pains. Pick the flowers at midday. Place in a clear jam jar and cover with sunflower oil. Leave in a sunny position, shaking daily and watch the oil turn bright red! After one month, strain off the herb. When rubbed onto the skin, the properties of the herb are absorbed into the bloodstream and act in the usual way.

N.B. If St Johns Wort is over-used it can increase sensitivity to the sun. Do not over-use if you are on allopathic medication including the contraceptive pill. Do not use if you are pregnant.

SUMMER SOLSTICE CELEBRATIONS

These are some suggestions for celebrating the Summer Solstice.

The eve of Summer Solstice is a special night to be out and often warm enough to sit out or go for a night walk. Walk in silence and connect to the mystical wild part of yourself which links with the Earth at this, one of the most ancient rites of transformation and rebirth. Sit around the fire and tell stories and music.

If possible, find a hill or high point from which to watch the Solstice Sunrise as it rises in the North East. Gather with like-minded folk at the stone circles. It begins to get light quite a while before the Sun actually comes up, and it's a good time to walk, listen to the birds and watch the colours come back into the world. Celebrate the Sun as its first rays appear. Give thanks for your achievements, hopes and aspirations.

Invite friends to gather on Solstice Eve. Prepare an area for feasting, performance and ceremony. Decide where to have the fire and where to pile up the firewood. Get the lanterns ready for when it gets dark later. Create a shrine to honour the Solstice. Decorate with pots of herbs and flowers and Sun images.

Pick lots of grasses, reeds, flowers, herbs, oak leaves, mistletoe, willow, and with ribbons and wool, people can weave them into garlands, girdles or headdresses for the celebration.

Light the Need-fire using twigs of oak and due ceremony. Once the fire has a good base of heat, burn oak wood, which will burn hot but slowly. Throw in herbs such as lavender and rosemary.

Begin by gathering into a circle, drum or create a simple chant all can sing together. Build up the power and feel yourself as part of the cycle of the solar year reaching a peak of intensity like the Sun. Lead the circle into a procession and circle the fire three times.

Honour the Five Elements in turn, with either one person or a person for each element leading each element and encouraging everyone to join in.

Fire in the South

Fire, the vital energy, has reached its peak with the Summer Solstice Sun. This is a moment of pause, to celebrate all we have achieved and all we have bought out into the light. The Sun brings energy and energises our wildest dreams and hopes! What are they? Give thanks for all that has been achieved and is yet to be achieved! Give thanks for transformation and change! Give thanks for what has been energised! Give thanks for spontaneity! celebration! our wild selves!

Water in the West

We give thanks for Water and bless the rain which is needed to swell the grain and that keeps the Earth refreshed and the crops alive. We celebrate the wonderful harmony of outer expression and inner stillness. We give thanks for both the ebb and the flow of our lives, the balance and the harmony. May we let ourselves flow free, flow well and let our hearts open. May we let our feelings loose so that we can express ourselves more fully. Send your love and thanks to those you love and to those who love you.

Earth in the North

We give thanks for the Earth and all her abundant growth and beauty. We too express ourselves to our fullest power in the outer world. From here this manifestation will ripen on the inner levels as we seek the wisdom within. What do you celebrate? Call out everything that makes you happy in this moment. Celebrate all you have achieved since this time last year.

Air in the East

We give thanks for each breath that gives us life. We give thanks for clean air and the sharing of song and music. We give thanks for the great gift of communication, seen and unseen. We celebrate the power of positive thought and intelligence. We pledge to use it in the service of the Earth. We celebrate the winds of change and the new understanding of unity and interconnectedness that we share in this moment.

Spirit at the Centre

Within and without and ever-present, we give thanks for this vital connection to this essential part of ourselves which cannot be seen and cannot be named. We reach out and in, connecting to our source and inner peace. May our outer achievements become part of our spiritual understanding and inner work.

The words I have written here are intended as clues, and pathways to understanding. When invoking the elements, it is important to speak from the heart and with power, so that you help to make the connection strong for yourself and all those present. Use the elemental charts on pages 30-34 to help you.

Celebrate this peak of fulfilment. Each share what they have gained since the Winter Solstice, and what they hope for in the coming months. This helps to honour and prepare for change. Focus on what still needs to be achieved before the inner cycle fully takes hold.

Celebrate the new phase of the year, the descent into the mysteries, the Summer lands. Understand that something must die in order to be reborn. This is the power of the dark, bringing transformation and renewal. It ripens on the inner levels all the things we are manifesting now.

The joining of Sun and the rain, Fire and Water, the conscious and the unconscious will complete the harvest, the Earth's as well as ours. Collect wool of blues and dark colours and wool of yellow, orange and red. Make a circle of people and on one side give the blue/dark wools, on the other give the sunny coloured wools. Each person with a ball of wool ties it loosely around their waist and then throws it across the circle to someone else who wraps it around their waist once, and then throws it to someone else in the circle, and so on. The interwoven colours created thus, symbolize the merging of energies. At the end, everyone can carefully step out of the web and it can be laid on the ground with night-lights in jars, placed around the outside.

Pass round a cup of honey mead, considered by the Druids to be a divine solar drink. Elderflower cordial or any fruit cup may be used. Salute the Sun and her gifts. Each say what you thank the Sun and this moment for as the Spirit moves you.

Carry effigies of the Corn Mother or fire dragons in a carnival procession. Wear masks and bright clothes. Dance, drum, and celebrate! Take circular paths, spiralling in and out. Carry lanterns. Celebrate yourself at the height of power and potential. Celebrate the dark. Welcome the change in direction.

Place the effigies from the procession central to the feasting and drama area. People may like to place posies of flowers by them, light candles for them. This way they are taken into the heart, becoming assimilated and understood.

Light a celebratory fire and create enough room for people to leap the fire. As you leap over the fire, call out what you give thanks for. By giving thanks you begin to recognise the gifts held within them and this transforms your relationship to them. Call out, "I give thanks for..." as you jump the fire. All offer encouragement and support to each other. Use the power of the fire to cleanse and purify, to let go of the old and anything that needs releasing. Call out, "I let go of..." Jump the fire as many times as you need to! This will help you move into the new phase. Express yourself fully so that you may move on.

Place aromatic herbs in the fire and expose yourself to the smoke. Traditionally, fennel, lavender, geranium, rue, rosemary, and chamomile were used.

Have a fire show if you know anyone who can give one. Light fireworks, especially Catherine wheels, or any fiery wheels that can be safely lit.

The Midsummer feast is a great social occasion that brings a community together. Now is a moment to shine, express your own uniqueness and enjoy each other's company and qualities. Look for the best in everyone.

This is the time for marriages. Couples who pledged themselves at Beltain, now become joined. An old custom was to hold a stick either side of the fire, each holding one end, and passing back and forth through the fire three times. 'Handfasting' joins the couple for a year and a day as they pledge themselves to each other. It is open to renewal every year. Gifts are exchanged and friends gather to witness and bless the occasion.

All drama began as sacred drama or magical drama, and was performed for understanding great truths and to bring enlightenment. They followed seasonal themes. The myths, legends and folk stories that have been handed down to us provide a wealth of material and inspiration. Here at the Summer Solstice, explore the themes of the solar wheel, the mystery of renewal, death and rebirth. Perform in the round. Use masks and make good use of candlelight and fire. Weave a spell of colour, sound and movement, allowing the audience to enter into the sacred dream world where perceptions change and reality shifts.

Make up your own circular dance patterns. It helps to keep it very simple in units of two or three repeated sequences. Establish the pace with one main drummer. There are always people who want to play percussion and the rhythm quickly swells with sound and energy. The Antic-Hey was an old dance danced at the Midsummer Solstice. 'Antic' meaning ancient, of the old religion, venerable, and 'Hey' meaning a figure of eight pattern on the ground – the infinity symbol of the Hindu/Arabic numeral system. 'Hey nonny nonny' was the call for the dance.

Tugs of war were a tradition of this time. You will need a long stout rope. On one side, all the people who were born in the summer, and on the other side, all the people who were born in the winter. This was the battle of summer and winter.

The ashes of the fire can be taken and used for any ceremonial purposes, or sprinkled around plants and herbs. Traditionally pieces of half burnt oak wood were put in the ground for fertility of the crops and also kept in the home to ward off lightning.

Whatever ceremony you began with to celebrate the Summer Solstice, you will need to bring the occasion to its conclusion with a closing ceremony. Thank the five elements for their energy. Thank the Sun and the Moon. Thank all of nature and all the guardians and spirit guides, the ancestors and nature spirits, and the spirits of the place. Thank the energy of Solstice to transform and energise! Thank each other.

Bless the food and drink. Feast and party.

LAMMAS

SUMMER CROSS QUARTER FESTIVAL

End July/Beginning August

MID-LEO ♌ FIXED FIRE

*Lammas Eve * Lughnasadh*
*Lugnnasa * Feast of Lug*
*The Feast of Bread * Loaf Mass*

Celebration of the Grain Mother

Festival of First Fruits
and Reminder

The Festival of Gathering In

LAMMAS

*Lammas is a celebration of the summer and the
gathering in of the grain harvest. This was
especially significant in the past. After all
the hard work of getting the grain crop
cut, threshed, stored and stacked, there
came a time for feasting, celebration
and assessment. Lammas is a Saxon
name meaning 'Loaf-mass'. Lughnasadh
(pronounced Loo-nas-ah) is Irish Gaelic.
On Lammas Eve fires were lit on Lammas
mounds such as Silbury Hill at Avebury, to
honour the Corn Mother as she gives birth
to her harvest child, the Grain. This is the seed
that will bring next year's harvest as well as the grain
that will sustain life throughout the winter.*

THE MONTH OF AUGUST WAS THE MONTH OF THE GRAIN MOTHER. An 'augur' is
an old word for seer and meant 'increaser'. The great abundance of the Earth Mother
is reflected in the titles she was given at this time: The Grain Mother, Barley Mother,
Corn Mother, Demeter, Ceres, Cerealia, Grain, the Wise One of the Earth, the
Increaser, She who is the seed, who is the womb, who is the soil, the Great Provider,
the Preserver of Life.

Cutting the 'corn' seems to be a general term for all cereal crops, whether they are
wheat, barley, rye or oats. There were many customs and rituals throughout Europe
to honour the first and the last sheaf of corn to be cut. The last sheaf was often cut by
the youngest girl present and fashioned into a Corn Maiden. It was carried joyfully
back to the village, sometimes plaited and decked with ribbons, and usually hung over
the fireplace. Sometimes it was dressed in women's clothes, and ritually burnt on the
Lammas Fire. Sometimes these Corn Maidens were kept until Yule when they were
divided up amongst the cattle or kept until the spring. Sometimes they were kept with
the date tied to them. Many Corn Maidens would be seen hanging above the fireplace.
In Scotland the 'young maid' was made out of the last stalks cut, and kept. The 'old

wife' was made out of the first stalks cut and was passed on to the nearest farm that had not finished bringing in the corn. This was then passed round until it ended up at the last farm to be cut. Another old European custom was to weave the last sheaf into a large Corn Mother with a smaller corn doll inside it, representing next year's unborn harvest.

The regenerative power of the Earth is never more manifest than now as the grain harvest is gathered in and the Sun's cycle begins to wane. The Cauldron of Regeneration was central to Celtic spiritual understanding. We are renewed by sleep and darkness, through many deaths and rebirths, and by the sacrifice of our outer lives for the inner journey. Here at Lammas, the doorway to the inner realms is opening. This is the symbolism behind the Demeter/Kore/Persephone story. Demeter, the Corn Mother, represents the ripe corn of this year's harvest, and Kore or Persephone represents the grain-seed who lives in the dark throughout the winter and reappears in the Spring. Persephone's descent into the Underworld is a mythical interpretation of the seed lying in the ground during the dark winter months, and her reappearance as the young maid, or the new sprouting seed, in the spring. This story shows us the Triple Goddess in all her aspects: as Earth Mother, the abundant provider; as the Crone, the wisdom found within; and as the Maiden who returns renewed in the spring. Pluto/Hades' abduction of Persephone is a later reworking of this older myth. After all the manifest energy and activity of the early summer, it is good to make time now to rest and to assimilate all that has happened during the Sun's active phase.

Lammas celebrations would probably have begun with the cutting of the last sheaf of corn. Although the 2nd of August is the calendar date for Lammas, the great Lammas fairs and feasts would probably have lasted from mid July to mid August and would have peaked around the time of the harvest Full Moon. Once the grain had been safely gathered in and the men returned from their hunting trips, it was a time for feasting, dancing and merry-making, a great celebration of the first of the harvest and assessment of the year's achievements. Beer, wine, cider and whisky made from the previous year's harvest, were ritually drunk, celebrating the transformative power of Fire and Water. Cooking fires were honoured as they too embodied the power of Fire and Water. Bread was made from the new grain and thanks were given to the Sun's life energy reborn as the bread of life.

Lammas is a time for tribal gatherings, a traditional time for travelling fairs, horse fairs (in honour of Rhiannon, the horse goddess of the Underworld), trading fairs of all kinds, markets, business transactions of all kinds, ritual games, horse racing, trial marriages (handfasting). The choosing of a new tribal leader would have taken place now as assessment and review of the active part of the year (and success of the crop) was undertaken. In the North of England these fairs are known as the 'Wakes'. They are still celebrated today, although they have lost touch with their roots, which included mourning for the death of the Sun.

Lugh or Lug was a Celtic god, a Sun king who, according to the myth, dies now with the waning year. He is John Barleycorn whose energy has gone into the grain, is cut down and sacrificed back to the land. This is the key to understanding Lammas, through the death and transformation of the Sun. We too, like the Sun, must sacrifice ourselves and the active outer energy of the year, and welcome the inner journey. In the Pagan tradition this is often interpreted as the sacrifice of the male ego, a giving way to the feminine power. But we must look beyond this to understand the energy shift we must all make from the potential of the active (referred to in the past as male) phase, to the potential of the receptive and regenerative (referred to in the past as female) phase, irrespective of our gender.

As we become more whole and learn to balance both sides of ourselves, the sacrifice of the active outer energy at this time becomes crucial to our well-being. Our modern lifestyle has forgotten the power and necessity of the Cauldron of Regeneration that the Celts understood as so important. Here at Lammas, we can make the necessary adjustments to turn and face our inner journey. We will carry our personal harvest through the darkness of winter, understanding it further on the deeper levels, until it is reborn and becomes manifest again in the spring.

THE UNDERLYING ENERGY OF LAMMAS

LAMMAS IS THE SEASONAL PEAK of high summer, and as
with all Cross Quarter festivals, it represents a change in the
manifest energy. Summer feels as if it will last forever, but now
we begin to see the first signs of change and transformation. In
the fields the cereal crops have turned from green to gold and
are gathered in. The first fruits, nuts and seeds are ripening and
we must think about what we wish to gather in, such as seeds
and plant medicines that will see us through the winter. This is
a time to make the most of the fine long days, travel about, have
adventures and walk the land.

Here we begin to assimilate and gather in our own harvest, the
first fruits of our active phase now manifest in the outer world
– the harvest of our hearts' desires, and the fruits of our labours.
This is a period of assessment as we begin to gather ourselves
together again after much scattering of energy. This is often a
holiday period, and gives us time to take a reflective look at
ourselves. In the spring we planted the seeds of our hopes, our
dreams and ourselves. Some things may have manifested and
some not. The Lammas assessment helps us to have a deeper
understanding of our actions and our selves at this point in time.

At Lammas we count our blessings and give thanks for all that
we are harvesting. Being aware of them will help us to see ways
to take them forwards into the next part of the cycle.

Full Moon in Aquarius

What is this coming through the Fire?
What is this spell in the song?
What is this star burning brighter?
What is this? What is this?

There's a rise in the eyes of the Gods of the forest,
There's a swell in the heart of the Gods of the sea
Sky-fliers swim in the winds of the wanting
And the Goddess flame burns ready
Inviting footprints on a path to the dawn
Bewitching steps across a leaping fire
Arms outstretched in the love of the moment
In the yell of the yelling and the breath of desire.

It's a rising tide of a new generation
Swelling sea of a storm to come
Shiver in the leaves on a fine Summer dawn
Echo of the future in the tribal drum
Full Moon in Aquarius

Brian Boothby
Tomorrows Ancestor

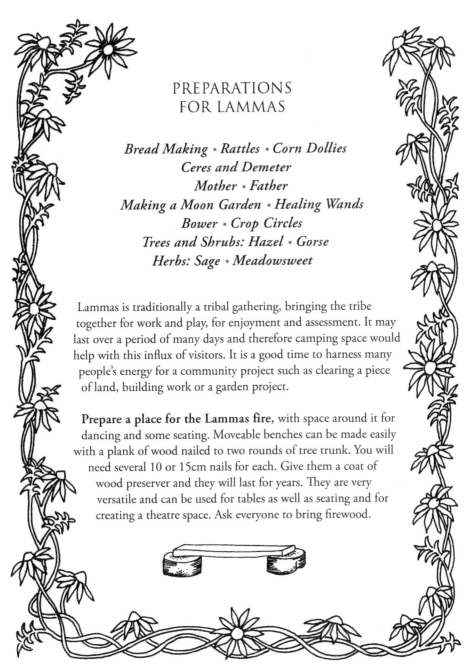

PREPARATIONS
FOR LAMMAS

Bread Making ∗ *Rattles* ∗ *Corn Dollies*
Ceres and Demeter
Mother ∗ *Father*
Making a Moon Garden ∗ *Healing Wands*
Bower ∗ *Crop Circles*
Trees and Shrubs: Hazel ∗ *Gorse*
Herbs: Sage ∗ *Meadowsweet*

Lammas is traditionally a tribal gathering, bringing the tribe
together for work and play, for enjoyment and assessment. It may
last over a period of many days and therefore camping space would
help with this influx of visitors. It is a good time to harness many
people's energy for a community project such as clearing a piece
of land, building work or a garden project.

Prepare a place for the Lammas fire, with space around it for
dancing and some seating. Moveable benches can be made easily
with a plank of wood nailed to two rounds of tree trunk. You will
need several 10 or 15cm nails for each. Give them a coat of
wood preserver and they will last for years. They are very
versatile and can be used for tables as well as seating and for
creating a theatre space. Ask everyone to bring firewood.

Prepare an area for the Lammas feast. An outdoor feast is very central to this celebration. Ask everyone to bring food to share and set up some tables for this. Provide sleeping mats, carpets and rugs so that the children can lie in their sleeping

bags when tired. Decorate the area with flags, bunting, and sheaves of grasses, wheat, oats, rye or barley tied up with red ribbon.

Weave and fashion a large Grain Mother from a bundle of grasses and flowers. As you weave and plait the stalks, give thanks for the grain harvest and share with each other all that this means to you.

Weave and plait smaller corn dollies from wheat or grass stalks. A single plait or concertina can be used to create simple shapes that can be hung up. As you plait and weave, focus on your own harvest. Look into your heart and celebrate all you have to be grateful for and for the hidden blessings held within the more difficult aspects of your harvest.

Create a Lammas shrine and ask everyone to bring something for it. If you have enough space, you can place this within an area created for contemplation and meditation. A circle of stones 4.5m across or a circle of bent willow or hazel rods is enough to define a space. Use a lump hammer and a metal spike to make holes in the ground and push in the thick end of the rod. Space the rods 30-60cm apart, bending them over and weaving the tops in the usual way. This could easily be created on a lawn, as it is impermanent and leaves just a circle of small holes

If you wish to turn this into something more permanent, use freshly cut willow-rods, keep them well watered and leave them over the winter. By the spring they will be growing well and can be woven and clipped to create a living willow hedge or dome.

Finish off the outdoor projects you began this summer, while you still have the energy and the light.

Plan a Lammas pilgrimage; to a local power spot, a stone circle, barrow, well, woods, or high point. Make a day of it. Take some bread, spring water and some fruit. Experience the changes in the Earth and in yourself. Look for ripening seeds to collect now or later, the first blackberries and the first hazelnuts falling; bring them back for your shrine.

Contemplate and assess your own harvest. Did the seeds that you planted at Imbolc grow as you had hoped? Are they the same dreams you wish to take with you through the incubation period of winter? Do not be disappointed if they have not yet materialised. Keep the vision strong and all things will come, perhaps when you least expect it and in ways which also may not be apparent at first. Perhaps there is a sacrifice to be made in order to achieve your heart's desire! True sacrifice is not giving up your own desires for others, but the sacrifice of a lower ideal for a higher one.

Meditate on the seed inherent within your harvest. Make time for meditation. State your readiness to receive inspired guidance, and let your intuition guide you. Take time to look at your life. What is its purpose or reason? How can you best serve humanity? How can you be of service to help the Earth? Much damage has been done. Industry and intensive farming has brought much pollution and destruction to natural resources, environments and the climate. Now we have a new threat with genetically modified crops that bear no seed and are the product of a world that has lost touch with nature and the natural cycles of the Earth. Pledge to support organic growers, whose farming methods care for the Earth and the environment.

Make a Rattle

A rattle filled with seeds, represent new life and can be used in any ceremony for renewing energy. Ideally use a natural gourd. Alternatively join two clean dry yogurt pots or tin cans together with tape. Make sure they are perfectly dry or the seeds will go mouldy. Add grain or other seeds. Different seeds make different sounds. Experiment with the sound. The sound will become dull if you put too many seeds in, and will stay 'lively' with less. It depends on what sound you like. When you are satisfied with the sound, Sellotape it together well and cover the whole thing with a couple of layers of newspaper strips glued on with watered-down PVA glue. When it is dry, paint with a base coat of household emulsion and then using acrylic paint on a design of your choice.

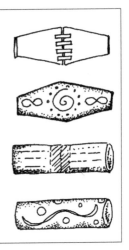

Look for seeds in the countryside or in friends' gardens that you can collect and dry, ready for sowing in the spring. Put them on paper to dry in a warm dry place, and then store them in envelopes, labelling them carefully.

Make a Moon Garden

This is a place to sit outside especially at the Full Moon and at the New Moon. It need only be a small area but with planning and intent, it will become a very special place in your garden for contemplation and meditation and to sit outside under the stars. It needs to be a sheltered spot, but as the Moon's place in the sky changes throughout the year and the night, it also needs to be open to the sky, possibly raised. A small seat or stone in each of the four directions will help your orientation to the Moon's place in the sky. A large flat stone in the centre can be used to put special things on, and as a place to put crystals to charge in the moonlight. Place a mirror face upwards at Full Moon. Place a glass bowl filled with spring water on the mirror and let it stand out all night under the Full Moon. In the morning add a quarter to half part brandy to your Moon water to preserve it. Take drops as needed to invoke Full Moon qualities. Plant white flowers, scented night flowers, aromatic herbs and plants associated with the Moon.

Ceres and Demeter

Demeter's spirit was believed to be in the first and last sheaves of the corn to be cut. It was called the Demeter, the Corn Mother, and the Old Woman. Kore, Ker or Persephone was the aspect of the Triple Goddess who descended into the Underworld for renewal and was reborn in the spring.

Ceres or Cerealia was the Latin (Roman) form of the Great Mother Goddess, the Grain Mother, Mother Earth, the dispenser of natural law. She was called 'Ceres Legifera', Ceres the lawgiver, and was the founder of the Roman legal system. The Greeks called her Demeter. 'Meter' means Mother, and 'De' is delta or triangle, the female genital sign. She was known as the abundant Mother, the Barley Mother, 'The Wise One of the Earth', 'She Who Is the Mother of the Seed'. The Great Mother Goddess was worshipped before the patriarchal religions began to supplant her. Country people, especially, continued to honour her despite the desperate measures the church took to stop them during the witch-hunt years.

The Mother

In ancient times all temples were dedicated to the Mother. The Earth was seen as a womb and our relationship to her that of a child to a mother. The Mother aspect of the Triple Goddess was seen as a bridge which linked the active manifest energy and the inner world. The Earth Mother was 'The Great Provider' bringing fertility, growth, nurturing abundance, harvest and community. Mother Earth, mother love, mother instinct, all reflect this link. Her colours are red, orange and gold.

In ancient times, when it was your birthday, you honoured your mother who gave birth to you. Motherhood is a sacred gift. We need to reclaim its power and its worth, to see it as an important time for nurturing and teaching your own and other people's children. Here at Lammas when the Earth Mother is honoured, we can use it to celebrate the mother within us, and our own mothers, whether they are alive or not. If you have no children of your own, then aim to spend time with friends' children. Build up lasting and meaningful relationships with children you know. We each have much to teach them and sharing time with children brings pleasure and benefits far into the future.

The Father
Many people claim a disconnection from their fathers or lack a deep and meaningful emotional relationship. It is generally agreed that there is much healing work to be done here. So much damage has been done by the patriarchal religions and by sending men off to fight wars. For many generations men have been encouraged to suppress their emotions and not to acknowledge their deepest feelings. This has meant many men have become isolated and deny themselves a true relationship with their women and children, and also other men. Here at Lammas, honour your father, whether he is alive or not, and fatherhood. Honour your relationship with your male children and with other people's male children, if you do not have children of your own. If you are male, pledge your willingness to be more open to your emotional softness. Forgiveness and compassion open the doors to the heart. Here at Lammas, let us share in a vision, a process of discovery, assessment and positive affirmations towards a more balanced male of the future.

Here at Lammas the Sun king or Sun god is honoured before he too sacrifices his outer attributes and turns inwards. Logical and rational thought is now balanced by its complementary opposite: intuition and inner wisdom. Our present day western culture is in a state of imbalance because the majority of people do not listen to their inner voice or acknowledge their intuition. Here at Lammas we can reclaim this side of ourselves. There is a great opportunity now to remember the value of connecting to the dark, the hidden aspects of our deeper selves, our emotions, our intuition, our instincts and inner knowing.

Healing Wands
A healing wand can be used for meditation and drawing towards ourselves a particular energy of a tree; and as a focus for holding a healing intention or positive affirmation.

They can be used for energy balancing, working with the chakras or the acupuncture meridian points. You will find your own way to work with tree spirits. Keep your intuition flowing and your heart open. Do not underestimate the power and abilities of the trees. In the past they were revered for their sacred connection to humankind. They are still easy to communicate with and most wish to work with us. They are there whenever we need them for support and guidance. Spend time with trees by sitting with your back against their trunks, letting their stillness come to you and opening yourselves to receiving impressions. Toning and singing with them helps open our intuitive channels. Look for fresh wind-blown wood to make your healing wands. Wands can be any size or shape.

Crop Circles

Patterns in cereal crops have been appearing every summer in the South of England since the early 1970s and continue to defy acceptable explanation and logic. Since those early simple circles and concentric rings, the designs have evolved and developed. Each year new patterns appear: symbols of keys, pendulums, insectograms, mandalas, Moons, spirals, and many complex and perfectly formed geometric shapes, symbols and patterns. Many are huge and appear in the crop in a very short space of time, defying logic and rational thinking. Their appearance is often accompanied by electrical disturbances reported locally, a fine mist and other unexplained phenomena. The patterns are formed by the stems of the cereal crop being bent at the base (the crop continues to grow and ripen despite being horizontal) and is found lying in swathes all facing the same direction and in spirals. For those lucky enough to get to the crop circles early, their perfection is awe-inspiring, lying perfectly straight and un-trampled. Many people have told of physical and emotional phenomena connected to their experiences in these crop circles. Research and speculation continue as crop circles move us to mystery and delight. Perfectly in harmony with Lammas, they provide a catalyst for change and transformation, helping us to reflect on the unexplained and explore our intuitive response.

TREES AND SHRUBS OF LAMMAS

HAZEL – *Corylus avellana*

This is the ninth tree of the Celtic Tree Ogham: COLL. C. and is linked to inner wisdom. In Celtic legend nine nuts of wisdom fell from the hazel tree into the river. They were eaten by a magical salmon who absorbed all the wisdom and changed into a young girl. The transformation inherent at Lammas is hidden in this story. The visions we act upon now will change our future and transform our present. Spending time with hazel will help us to find inspired solutions and to follow an intuitive path rather than a well-thought-out plan. Look for areas of your life that you intuitively feel need changing and act upon inspired solutions. It is an easy tree to communicate with and has shared its long straight poles with humankind since ancient times. Hazel makes a fine walking stick and companion that will enhance other communication with non-verbal beings such as minerals, stones, trees, plants and animals. Go to the hazel when you need to overcome creative blocks and when seeking your own inner wisdom.

Making a Hazel Walking Stick

1. Cut yourself a hazel stick or staff, asking the tree first and choosing intuitively. Thank the tree for its gift.

2. Shape the top in what ever way feels right, first with a knife and then with rough sandpaper. Consider a shape that feels good to hold and when you are satisfied with this, bring out the smoothness of the wood with a medium and then fine sandpaper.

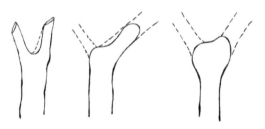

3. Sand the bark gently with a fine sandpaper to bring out the colours and patterns of it's beautiful bark and rub with any oil. Alternatively, strip the bark off and leave to dry out indoors. When it has dried, sand it down until it is smooth, beginning with rough sandpaper and ending with a fine one. Oil your stick with teak oil, linseed oil, or a beeswax polish.

Making a Healing Wand or Albion Pin

You can make a small healing wand which can be carried in your pocket. Use the same method as the walking stick on page 179.

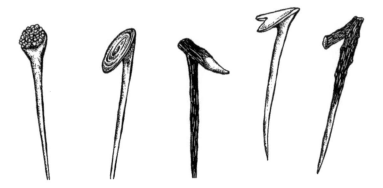

An Albion pin is worn to pledge allegiance to the tree spirits and the spirits of nature. It is made using a natural feature found in a twig or thorn, and sharpened to pin into the lapel of a jacket or hat band (but do NOT use Blackthorn thorns).

GORSE – *Ulex europaeus*

Although not a tree, the gorse is the seventeenth in the Celtic Tree Ogham: ONN.O. Gorse is found on moorland and common land and flowers for most of the year. In Celtic legend it is linked to wisdom that comes as a result of hard work, fruitfulness and fulfilment on the inner levels as well as in the outer world. Gorse is linked to Lammas as we harness the last energy of the waning year and reap the harvest of our hard work. For those who feel their harvest has not been a good one, the Bach flower remedy gorse will restore hope and faith in the future. Spend time with gorse and assimilate its vibration. Find yourself a gorse wand, and use it for counting your blessings and to focus on a positive path forward.

HERBS OF LAMMAS

This is a busy time for harvesting herbs and collecting herb seeds to sow in the spring. Give thanks and blessings as you pick them, dry them and store them. Review what you know about them and ways you can use them both physically and metaphysically.

SAGE – *Salvia officinalis*
Harvest sage at the end of July, before the flowers have come out. Sage is a herb associated with wisdom and releasing blocks in expression. It is connected to the throat chakra and is for those who have something to say but cannot let it out. It will help you express your emotions. Make the herb tea in the usual way. The infusion is a useful antiseptic herb for sore throats, laryngitis, tonsillitis, mouth ulcers and mouth infections. It can be used as a gargle, for bathing wounds, sores, and to stop bleeding. Use the tea infusion externally and then drink afterwards as well. It will dry up excess secretions such as catarrh or sinusitis. It contains oestrogen and is useful in the menopause and for delayed menstruation. Burn dried sage to cleanse and purify. Waft the smoke around a person to cleanse their aura (called smudging). This is a good way to begin any ritual or ceremony.

N.B. It must not be taken if pregnant, and because of its drying action, it must not be taken for long periods of time. It will dry up mother's milk. Care must be taken by those who are insulin-dependent, and to be avoided by epileptics.

MEADOWSWEET – *Filipendula ulmaria*
Garlands of meadowsweet were traditionally worn for the Lammas celebrations. Its heady perfume expands the psyche, and builds inner strength. It enhances flexibility and connection to the inner levels. It is a mild sedative and painkiller containing salicylic acid (aspirin) that affects the rate at which blood clots. It is a good digestive tonic that reduces excess acidity and is useful for heartburn, hyperacidity, gastritis and peptic ulcers. As it cleanses the body of harmful acids, it is useful for any inflammatory conditions such as rheumatoid arthritis. It is a strong diuretic (increases urine) and can be used for any bladder or kidney complaint including cystitis. It reduces stagnation in the liver and therefore will help the immune system function more effectively. Its harvest time is July and August when the flowers are just beginning to open. Collect them in brown paper bags to dry for later use.

N.B. Avoid if on anti-coagulant drugs.

LAMMAS CELEBRATIONS

These are some suggestions for celebrating Lammas.

Invite friends for a bring-and-share feast and Lammas gathering. Plan to have a fire and invite musicians to play.

Make time to be outside and appreciate the peak of summer. Sense the changes that are coming. Prepare yourself for the waning energy of the Sun and how this will affect you. Gather grasses, herbs and flowers for weaving into garlands and headbands for the Lammas celebration. As you weave, think about your own harvest that you are reaping now and how you can facilitate this further. Look beyond the outer harvest that is manifested, to the harvest within. Every cloud has a silver lining. Everything that happens to you can be seen in a positive light. Count your blessings.

Ask a local farmer for a sheaf of oats, wheat, barley or rye. Failing that, gather armfuls of long grasses. Use this for weaving a Corn Mother and for smaller corn dollies and other woven corn mementoes. Weave in flowers and herbs and decorate with red, orange and gold ribbons. This could be something to help bring focus to the Lammas theme, as people arrive.

Weave a headband or garland of grasses and flowers
to wear at the Lammas ceremony. Bind a circle of
grass together and tie with grass or a pale coloured
garden string. Weave in flowers and herbs.

Bread Making and Seed Biscuits

Bake your own bread and biscuits with seeds and nuts in them. As you do this, give thanks for the grain harvest that makes this possible and the seed within the harvest. Celebrate the Earth's abundance. Pledge to support organic farming that respects the Earth. Making bread is very relaxing and easy and children love to make their own rolls. Eating the bread afterwards is the final treat! The 'quick' yeasts in sachets require only one ten minute knead. (Follow the instructions on the packet.) To make plaited loaves, make three long rolls of dough and plait in the usual way. Place the plaited loaf on a warm greased baking tray. Cover with a clean tea towel and leave in a warm place to rise (about one hour). Bake in a hot oven for 15-20 minutes. Small rolls can be made in the same way and only need baking for 10 minutes. Experiment with different shapes and added extras such as dried fruit, nuts, olives, and sunflower seeds.

Lammas Bower

Create a bower or four-way archway with four hazel poles joined in the middle. Each pole can be orientated to each of the four directions. Each pole can be decorated by tying on bunches of flowers and grasses. The children love helping to do this. In the centre on a golden cloth, place the Corn Mother you have made and all around, place the food which represents the grain harvest: bread, cakes, biscuits. Include vases of flowers, hedgerow fruit and nuts and edible fungi. Hang red ribbons from the top and any other corn creations. Make it look beautiful, a true celebration of the grain harvest and first fruits.

Bring the group together into a circle round the bower. Light a candle at each of the directions; place something at each one representing each element. Honour Spirit at the centre and around the outside of your circle. 'Smudge' the area with burning sage, coltsfoot, or lavender. As you smudge, state clearly your intent of cleansing the space and raising awareness during the ceremony. In the centre of the bower, place three large candles: one green to represent the Earth in her spring green colour, one gold to represent the Earth in her harvest colour, and one purple or black to represent the Earth as she moves inwards for the winter. Light these with ceremony, honouring the three aspects of the Earth as you light them. Bring the group together with a chant to honour the Earth Mother.

Make a circle around the bower by holding hands. Walk or dance around it, first clockwise to the right, and then widdershins to the left. Focus on the turning direction of the year as you dance, if you are celebrating on your own, dance around the bower and honour the Five Elements in turn.

Honour the Five Elements. This can be done by everyone, each speaking their truth in the moment. Alternatively five people agree to represent each of the Elements. Towards the end of the dance, they can take up their positions in the direction they are going to speak for. Each person should be dressed in the colours of that element, easily achieved with coloured scarves. Alternatively, if it is a public celebration, a few people can speak for each element and act as an echo for what is said. This helps the words to be heard. Do not read words but speak from the heart so that your words have strength and power. Agree on the order beforehand so that the ceremony flows.

Fire in the South

We honour and give thanks for the power of the Sun that has brought the harvest to fruition. We give thanks for the harvest of grain and first fruits. We give thanks for our own harvest and all we have learnt. May we understand this harvest on the many levels. At this time of Lammas we prepare for change and transformation as the outer growth is sacrificed and inner understanding becomes active.

Water in the West

We honour and give thanks for Water, for the rain that is needed to swell the grain and the fruits. We give thanks for the expansive flow and currents of the heart and emotions, which have been brought out into the light. Now the outward spiral begins to turn inward. We welcome reflection and trust our intuitive understanding. Now it is time to seek the healing and understanding from within.

Earth in the North

We give thanks to the Earth for the grain which will sustain life throughout the winter and the seeds which will bring next year's harvest. We give thanks for our abundance of food and grain for bread and cereals. We pledge to help those who do not have this abundance. We honour our mothers, our fathers, our friendships, our family, the children, our experiences and achievements this year, and all that has nurtured us and all we have nurtured. With assessment, the cycle is complete. We bless all that has been given, learnt and assimilated. We let go of things no longer needed. We give thanks for the hidden blessings yet to be revealed.

Air in the East

We give thanks for the abundance of communication, the gift of knowledge and our freedom to share information. We give thanks for all the experiences that have helped shape us, for new understanding and loving kindness that has grown in our hearts. Now we take a reflective look at ourselves and learn from our experiences. We welcome the seeds of our new beginnings, a new journey, as we turn inwards once again for renewal.

Spirit at the Centre

We give thanks for Spirit that nurtures and sustains us. Our achievements are a reflection of our connection to Spirit and the guidance we receive from within. We reconnect to our inner world and the still point of inner peace and ask that we can find new and inspiring ways to integrate this into our daily lives.

The words I have written here are intended as clues, and pathways to understanding. When invoking the elements, it is important to speak from the heart and with power, so that you help to make the connection strong for yourself and all those present. Use the elemental charts on pages 30-34 to help you.

Honour the Grain Mother and the harvest of the Earth. Give everyone an ear of wheat and let each one add it to the Grain Mother in the centre. Each person gives thanks to the Earth and her abundance as the Great Provider. We remember the people in the world who are hungry. How can we share our abundance with others? Focus now on how we can help heal this imbalance. A simple drumbeat or hum will help to focus this moment.

Feel yourself to be part of the abundance and fullness of the season. Share with each other what your personal harvest is. Lammas is the moment to assess where you are on your path. Give thanks for what you have gained in the outer world, and what you will take with you into the inner realms. Count your blessings. Being thankful for the things you have opens the doorway to your own abundance. Storing our blessings in our hearts means we can access them in the winter.

Now would be a good moment for a hand fasting, a baby's naming ceremony, a rite of passage, and any other ceremony that honours and celebrates the achievements of individuals and the community.

Look within to see what negative thoughts you may be nurturing. Look beyond them to the fear that lies behind them, and then beyond this to a loving positive solution. Acknowledging negativity and understand its purpose in your life. See it as a new beginning, an opportunity to transform it for your future happiness.

Make a 'Basket of Abundance'. Put something in from your summer harvest, and take out something that someone else has put in. Ask everyone to bring something for this purpose.

Honour your father and your mother or the people whom you acknowledge as being a father or mother to you, even if they are no longer alive. Ask everyone to bring a photograph of them. Pin them to the Corn Mother, thanking them for their positive qualities and forgiving them their negative qualities. Honour yourselves as mothers and fathers, or surrogate mothers and fathers. Honour the energy that you give to the children. Forgive yourself the mistakes you have made.

Dance a spiral dance, with one person leading the group into a large circle and then holding hands, spiralling evenly into the centre. When everyone has stopped and can go no further, tone notes of harmony, Om or Awen. The Celts called their Moon mother Omh – 'She Who Is'. Awen is a Welsh word meaning inspire, Spirit-flow. Let the sounds flow in one continuous sound bath lasting for at least ten minutes. As everyone is very close, the sound resonates and vibrates through everyone's bodies and is very powerful. After it is over, let each say, "thank you for..." as Spirit moves them. This facilitates a state of gratitude and radiance from within. When all is done, take up the same hand you held when you spiralled in (most important) and spiral out, smiling into each other's eyes.

Bless the food and drink brought to share. Feast and party.

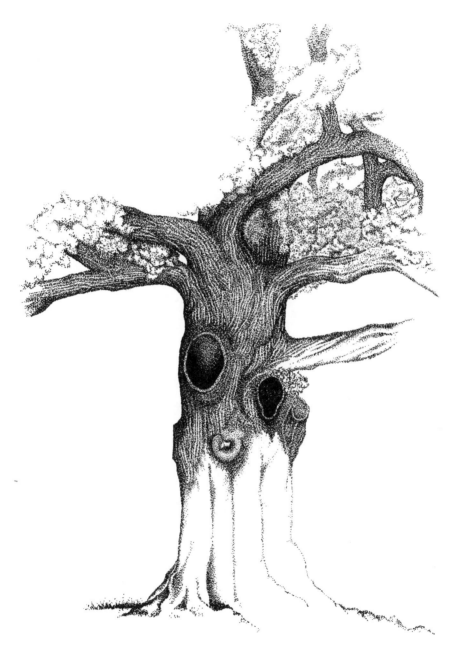

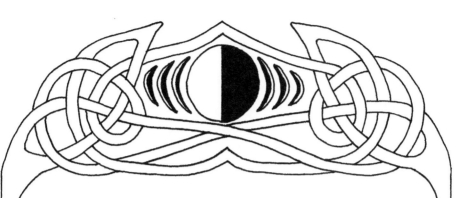

AUTUMN EQUINOX

AUTUMN QUARTER POINT

20th-23rd September

SUN ENTERS LIBRA ♎

Day and night equal length

*Mabon * Alban Elued*

Harvest Festival

Festival of Thanksgiving

*Festival of Restored Balance
and Integration*

AUTUMN EQUINOX

*Day and night are in perfect balance again all over the world.
The Sun enters the sign of Libra, bringing balance and
harmony and, by necessity, change and transformation.
It is time to take action and move into a new energy phase to
balance the outer world with the inner world. It is a time to
release the past and move forwards, a chance to be clear about
what it is you want to do now and prepare for winter.*

AUTUMN EQUINOX IS THE DOORWAY TO WINTER. Summer is over and a new phase
will begin. Here we can share with each other what we have gained and completed
during the summer and make our plans for the coming winter. From now on the days
will get noticeably shorter and colder. The Sun's power is waning fast. This is the time
of ripening fruits, nuts, mushrooms and berries. It is a busy time if you want to lay in
stores for the winter. After all is gathered in, and the outside jobs are completed, we
can celebrate the harvest. This is the family gathering of autumn's end, Thanksgiving,
the big harvest party; a feast and a celebration of the year's abundance. Here we
celebrate the Earth and all her gifts, friendships, family, our produce, our creations and
achievements, as well as our own personal harvest.

It is a time for balancing and reconciling opposites and to see them as part of the
whole. Everything co-exists together and we need both sides in order to be balanced
and whole: the seen and the unseen, the known and the unknown, creation and
destruction, death and rebirth, materialism and spirituality. Here at the Autumn
Equinox, celebrate your whole selves, your masculine and feminine aspects, your
conscious and unconscious, the active and the receptive, your light and dark sides,
your fortunes and your misfortunes, your young self and your old self – and all aspects
of the cycle of life. Celebrate it all, the good and the bad. Honour the changing
season that brings a chance to start again. Dragon Day was celebrated at the Spring
and Autumn Equinoxes. The dragon goes underground now for the winter. Here the
dragon is invoked to carry the Fire energy into the inner realms, to activate the Fire
within. The dragon is an ancient energy symbol representing Earth energy, dynamism,
Fire, will and courage. This we take with us now as we turn to face the dark inner
realms. This is not a place to fear as we have been taught, but a place to get in touch
with your power, strength, inner focus, spiritual path and a reconnection to your inner
wisdom. We are part of this whole, not separate from it.

THE UNDERLYING ENERGY
OF THE AUTUMN EQUINOX

THE EQUINOXES PREPARE US FOR CHANGE IN THE EARTH'S ENERGY. This is the transition into the winter season that we must all respond to. Things are moving fast now. Preparations and intentions for the coming winter months must be made now. The days are shortening and the increasing cold is here to remind us that change is coming. The leaves are changing colour and falling from the trees; the fruit is ripening and needs to be gathered in. Outside jobs need to be completed.
The sap in the trees and plants is moving down now.

This is the beginning of root energy and brings rest, sleep, and renewal. It is a chance for all of life to go within and re-enter the dark womb of the spiritual world. Equinox celebrates the balance between the outer journey and the inner journey, and the strong foundation this brings into our lives. It is a time for long-term planning and incubation. The seed ideas we plant now will re-emerge in the spring, changed, transformed and strengthened by their time in the unconscious. Use the Autumn Equinox to begin to turn inwards. Listen to the understanding and intuition that come from your inner knowing. Learn to trust this part of yourself and value the transformation inherent in this season.

Give thanks for your harvest. A state of gratitude opens your heart and increases the flow of Love and abundance in your life. Give thanks for the inner rewards you are beginning to harvest and look for ways to use them in the future. Ask for guidance; be open to a change in focus, or a change in direction in your life. State your intent to connect to your inner wisdom and to follow your spiritual path.

At this moment, when we appreciate all that the Earth has provided for us, ask yourself what you can give back, to help the healing of the Earth, to undo the damage of our industrial/ scientific age. The gift you have is your inspired vision and enlightenment; your love, compassion and higher ideals that

will affect all those you speak to, and will bring changes in the world. Welcome your awakening intuitive creative faculties that will help heal our imbalanced rational world. Share the wisdom and power this brings you. Manifest the goodness of your spirit in all you do.

The double spiral is the symbol of Autumn Equinox. It represents the in-breath and the out-breath; the point of balance between the worlds; the inner and outer journey. This endless cycle of change brings renewal and new opportunities to explore and understand our selves and the life we are creating. Your harvest is the starting point of this understanding. At the Autumn Equinox, look back with thanks and blessings to the gifts and help given, to the expansion that began in the spring. Welcome the turning, the change of energy flowing towards the dark and the power within. Connect to your inner pathways, your spiritual path. Rest, re-charge, and find the source of your inner world. Slip out of time. Dream a new dream.

Love for Life

I am so small and yet I'm always cared for,
My share of abundance awaits.
And your life is yours just for the cost of living it,
And even that is up to you.

Counting blessings
Thanking the land
Connecting to the source of Life

Opening hearts
In simple gratitude
Returning love for life

So sit on the hill, and watch the Sunrise,
Forget your hardships, break your bread.
We give so much – we give so little
The balance settles with gratitude.

Counting blessings
Thanking the land
Connecting to the source of Life

Opening hearts
In simple gratitude
Returning love for life

Returning love for life returning
Love for life returning
Love for life
Returning – Love for life

Brian Boothby
Tomorrows Ancestor

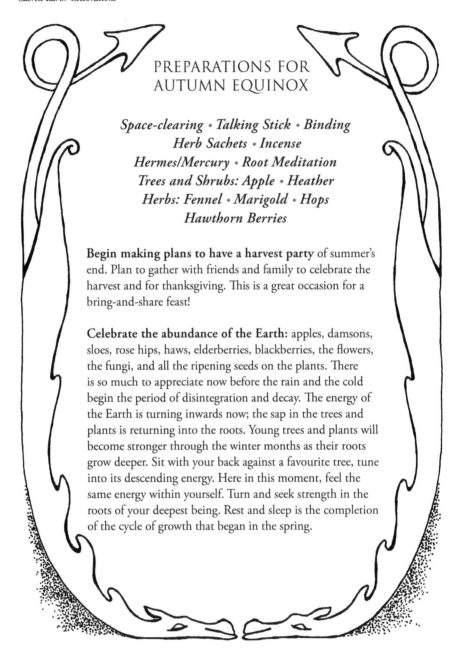

PREPARATIONS FOR AUTUMN EQUINOX

*Space-clearing * Talking Stick * Binding*
*Herb Sachets * Incense*
*Hermes/Mercury * Root Meditation*
*Trees and Shrubs: Apple * Heather*
*Herbs: Fennel * Marigold * Hops*
Hawthorn Berries

Begin making plans to have a harvest party of summer's
end. Plan to gather with friends and family to celebrate the
harvest and for thanksgiving. This is a great occasion for a
bring-and-share feast!

Celebrate the abundance of the Earth: apples, damsons,
sloes, rose hips, haws, elderberries, blackberries, the flowers,
the fungi, and all the ripening seeds on the plants. There
is so much to appreciate now before the rain and the cold
begin the period of disintegration and decay. The energy of
the Earth is turning inwards now; the sap in the trees and
plants is returning into the roots. Young trees and plants will
become stronger through the winter months as their roots
grow deeper. Sit with your back against a favourite tree, tune
into its descending energy. Here in this moment, feel the
same energy within yourself. Turn and seek strength in the
roots of your deepest being. Rest and sleep is the completion
of the cycle of growth that began in the spring.

Plant native tree seeds such as acorns from the oak, hazelnuts from the hazel, rowan berries from the rowan, alder cones from the alder, haws from the hawthorn. Label the pots and leave them outside without a saucer under them. Some will germinate in the spring, when they can be potted up into a larger pot. Some will take two years to germinate. Later you will need to find permanent homes for them. Plant them in the ground when the leaves have fallen and root energy begins.

Finish off any garden projects you may have started. Move trees, bushes and perennials to their new positions. Split herb plants and share them with your friends or replant in new positions. Clear the garden, cut back, weed and compost. Collect seeds for growing in the spring. Give thanks for the abundance you have enjoyed in your garden. Give thanks to the flowers, herbs and the medicines you have harvested. Give thanks to the nature spirits, retreating now.

Plant native bulbs in the ground where they will stay hidden until the spring. Plant mixed bulbs in large pots and stand them outside your door. This way you will see and appreciate their re-emergence as the light returns after the Winter Solstice.

There is much to do at this time, gathering fruit, making fruit wines, jams and preserves, collecting and drying mushrooms and seeds. This is a busy time in the kitchen that once again becomes the heart of the home. Prepare food for the feast using the abundance of the season. As you make the food, give thanks from your heart for all that you have.

Let the abundance of the Earth speak for itself. Collect autumn leaves and make a celebratory basket of coloured leaves. In other baskets collect nuts and seeds, seed-heads, fungi, fruits and berries. They can be displayed and honoured in any creative way you wish. Hang up coloured cloths of browns, yellows, oranges and reds.

Space Clearing

This is the time to clean out and clear your space ready for the coming new season. Throw out or give away unwanted things that are no longer relevant, or hold emotional associations that may be holding you back. Move forward into the new season with greater clarity, uncluttered by psychic dross. Creating light and harmony in your living space will greatly affect how you feel and what you achieve in your space. As you are about to move indoors now, the importance of a clean uncluttered space for yourself cannot be over-emphasised. Give everything a wash, getting rid of all the dust. Burn sage to cleanse the space. Create a special area or shrine to focus your spiritual journey. Light candles there. Put appropriate Bach flower remedies into water and, using a

195

plant-spray, spray the room to enliven and enhance its energy and your energy within it. As you work, state clearly your intent for clarity and harmony. It is a wonderfully uplifting thing to do and afterwards your room feels very different.

Dedicate an area of your room to your spiritual growth: a window ledge, a table, or a shelf. On it, place a coloured cloth, a vase of fresh flowers, crystals, and anything of significance that will help you keep connected to your spiritual path and the insights you are gaining. Light a candle here whenever you make this connection.

Wash all your crystals and put them under the harvest Full Moon to recharge. Thank them for all their help, for their energy, power and healing. Crystals are very powerful living things, acting directly on the energy field of the body. They respond to vibrations of respect, care and love, like all living things. They can help us to become balanced, to communicate with all of nature and to experience all life as sacred.

Make time for meditation and connection to your inner self. Meditate with the spiral, the double spiral, and the inner and outer breath. Seek to balance the busy outer world with the peace within. Nurture a sense of gratitude for all you have. This will open your heart to love and inner peace. Meditation will facilitate positivity, peacefulness and serenity. When it becomes a part of your daily life, it creates a balance between our active and receptive selves. Practise mindfulness meditation. This means keeping focused on the present as you go about your daily chores. As you become aware of your thoughts and what comes up from the unconscious, gently bring yourself back to the present moment and the job you are doing.

Herb Sachets and Herb Storage
Sort out your dried herbs, throwing away last year's unused leaves and flowers. (Roots may be kept for two years if they still smell good.) Make sure that this year's herbs are properly dried, labelled and stored in a dry place in dark jam jars or brown paper bags. Sunlight and damp will destroy their properties. Using circles of muslin and coloured threads, tie herbs into herb teabags or herb bath sachets (See page 152.) Make a note of the herbs in them and label them. Give some to friends as gifts.

Incense Making
Experiment with different incense mixtures of dried herbs, berries and flowers. Keep a note of what you put into the different mixtures and what you might use them for. Give the mixtures your own special names, label and store them in a dry place. Burn the dried mixture in a special dish using glowing charcoal blocks.

Making a Talking Stick

Make a talking stick that can be passed around the group to facilitate discussion, share deep thoughts and feelings. The person who holds the stick is the only one who can speak and must not be interrupted. When she or he has finished speaking, it is passed on to the next person who wishes to speak. It is a power stick and can greatly focus and aid communication. It can take many forms. It may be a piece of wood you find, or one you cut, with thanks and intent. A good size is 40-60cm long and 2-3cm in diameter. But there are no fixed rules. You may prefer to leave the bark on or strip off the bark, sand it smooth and polish with beeswax polish or oil. Oiling it will keep the wood strong and stop it from drying out and cracking. You can also bind coloured threads on to it.

1. Tie a length of thread on your stick, with one long thread that runs the length of the stick and stays inside the binding.

2. Wrap the wrapping thread round the stick, carefully laying each wrap snuggly against the last and keeping the inner thread inside the binding. Change colours by tying on a new colour to the wrapping thread, carefully binding the knots inside, and continue to keep the inner thread running inside the binding.

3. Tie off by tying the wrapping thread to the thread that ran inside. Tie on bells, shells, stones with holes in, feathers, beads and other special things.

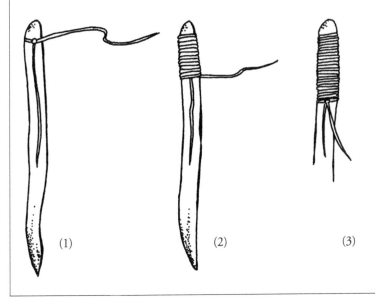

(1)   (2)   (3)

Seek to balance the male and female within yourself. Take a look at your life and perhaps notice areas where you are still responding to your conditioning and what society is expecting of you. Find ways to change so that you feel more balanced within your self.

At the Spring and Autumn Equinoxes, fast for a day to help cleanse the body of harmful toxins. Drink mineral water and herb teas (fennel is good) to aid the process.

Hermes (Greek)/Mercury (Roman)

Worshipped extensively in the pre-Christian era as a four-fold god, his sign, the Arabic numeral four later became incorporated into the Christian cross. Hermes-Mercury was a god of the four elements, the four quarters of the Earth, the four winds, the four seasons, the four great Fire festivals, the four quarters of the year (Solstices and Equinoxes), the four fixed zodiac signs and animal totems of the year, and later the four archangels. Hermes-Mercury represents the blending of opposite forces, outer and inner, active and passive. His logical aspect, represented by the phallus or rod, was balanced by his intuitive aspect represented by the twin serpents, thus creating the caduceus, used in astrology and alchemy, as a symbol of healing. The serpents, dragons or snakes of Hermes-Mercury were sometimes shown in a circle biting their own tail, representing the unending cycle of death and rebirth. The hermetic power of androgyny and blended opposites is an ancient mystery whose potent symbolism has survived for us to re-examine.

Mercury is dedicated to communication, especially between the worlds. There were many temples dedicated to Hermes or Mercury, always to be found on high places. Many of these later became dedicated to the Archangel Michael, the angel of death and transformation. The two St Michael's Mounts, one in Cornwall and the other across the English Channel in France, were both Mercury's mounts in pre-Christian times. (The French one still bears the name St Michel – Mont Mercure.)

TREES AND SHRUBS OF AUTUMN EQUINOX

APPLE

The cultivated apple tree (*Malus pumila domestica*), and the crab apple (*Malus pumila*), both have similar properties and a long history of myths and legends, cures and uses. In every country it is regarded as sacred, magical, a symbol of fruitfulness and abundance, a means to immortality, a cure for all ills, and a gift of Love. It is the tenth tree of the Celtic Tree Ogham: QUERT. Q. From Greece to the British Isles, it is connected to the fabled Western Isles of immortality, and has strong links to the Underworld and inner journeying. Here at Autumn Equinox, it is a symbol of the Earth's abundance. It teaches us to give all, in total trust that all will be replenished. It inspires us to be open to our loving heart and to the abundance in our lives. By affirming and feeling thankful for what we have in the present, we open up the channels for our own abundance.

Apple is a powerful cleanser. The Bach flower remedy can be taken internally by those who have a poor self-image, and used externally, a few drops in the washing water to cleanse your outer body, room, utensils, or wherever you feel the need of its cleansing energy. It is used for psychic cleansing as well as physical.

Verjuice

Verjuice, the ancient magical drink of the Druids, is made by laying ripe crab apples in a heap until they begin to sweat. Remove the stalks and the rotten fruit, beat the remainder to a mash in a large bowl. Press this through a coarse cloth or muslin. Bottle the juice and leave for one month.

HEATHER – *Calluna vulgaris*

Heather is not a tree but is never the less included in the Celtic Tree Ogham. It is eighteenth in the Ogham: Ur. U. It is seen as a gateway between the inner world of spirit and the outer world of manifestation. How you go about your life is very much a reflection of your inner world, and demonstrates a loyalty to one's true self. If you are at peace with yourself, you will do what is right without ulterior thought of reward or advantage. This is the message of heather. Spending time with heather will lift the spirits and bring a calming soothing energy. Heather inspires us to go about our lives with this same lightness of spirit, which we can then pass on to others. Seek out any areas of your life that are causing you stress and find inspiring ways to increase your inner peace. Collect the flowers for herb teas. Frequently used in cleansing mixtures, it is a diuretic and antiseptic.

HERBS OF AUTUMN EQUINOX

FENNEL – *Foeniculum vulgare*

Harvest the seeds in the autumn. Make an infusion in the usual way and use for all gastric disturbances, for stimulating digestion, reducing bloating and helping to expel wind. Fennel is a hot dry herb and will get rid of dampness and cold. It can be safely drunk by nursing mothers to increase milk production, passing through the mother's milk to the baby to reduce wind and colic. Fennel is nourishing and sustaining, whenever you feel you need nurturing. It has a soothing calming effect on the emotions.

N.B. It is a uterine stimulant, so use sparingly if pregnant.

HOPS – *Humulus lupulus*

Harvest the hop flowers in early September as they cascade over the hedgerows. Hang them up to dry as part of your Equinox decorations. It is a strong sedative, calming the liver and the stomach, relieving headaches and sleeplessness due to stress. Mix dried hop flowers and lavender flowers and fill a small cotton pillow with this mixture. Sleep with the herb pillow inside the pillowcase to ease insomnia.

N.B. Do not use hops if you are feeling depressed, as they will make the depression worse.

MARIGOLD – *Calendula officinalis*

A herb of the Sun to take with you into the winter. The petals can be gathered in September and dried for winter use as herb tea. It is a powerful blood cleanser that works on the lymphatic system and builds up the immune system. Drink the infusion whenever the immune system is lowered, and for viral and fungal infections such as candida. The same infusion can be used to bathe wounds, and is safe to use with children and babies. Calendula will bring comfort to the spirit. It has a soothing effect after shock, trauma or anger. The fresh leaves and petals can be added to salads.

HAWTHORN BERRIES – *Crataegus monogyna*

Collect and dry the haws from September to October. This is the primary remedy for all problems of the heart. It should be drunk regularly in later life to relieve and prevent angina, hardening of the arteries, and palpitations of the heart, water retention and poor circulation. It will regulate high or low blood pressure, depending on the need, and gently bring the heart back to normal function, improving the general condition of the heart. It is also a useful herb for relieving stress, insomnia and any nervous condition. Pour cold water onto a handful of berries and let them stand overnight, strain and drink the next morning. The berries can be burnt as an incense to help release blocked energy and open the heart to giving and receiving love. By releasing stress, it enhances a person's ability to let go and trust.

AUTUMN EQUINOX CELEBRATIONS

These are some suggestions for celebrating the Autumn Equinox.

Plan to get out and about and experience the Equinox on the day whatever the weather. The exact time and day can be found in any astrological diary. (See Recommended Reading page 234.) Bring back treasures from your walk to put on your Autumn Equinox shrine.

Gather with friends and family for a bring-and-share feast. Ask everyone to bring food and drink that reflects the season. By putting tables together and covering them with sheets, it may be possible to seat everyone for a real communal feast with much toasting and dedications, thanking the Earth and each other. Decorate the tables with vases of flowers, fruit, nuts and autumn leaves. Light candles with a dedication and thanks for the harvest of the year. Before you eat, bless the food. Say a simple grace together. You will need to decide whether to feast first, or have the ritual celebration first, how to balance and harmonise the two, and how to use the space available creatively.

Thanksgiving and balance are the twin themes of the Autumn Equinox. Seek to take the harvest you have gained in the outer world and integrate it with the turning within, to help bring clarity to the way ahead as the season changes from autumn to winter.

Have some baskets of yarns, seeds, shells, string, sticks, fir cones, feathers, dried grasses, dried flowers, ribbons, threads, needles, scissors. Ask everyone to bring something and then sit together, weave, thread, bind, create something that reflects the abundance of the moment. It may be a necklace to wear, a headdress, an autumn posy to hang up, a special wand or totem. As you make it, think positively about what you are harvesting and how you can use this for your greater good and the greater good of the Earth.

Set aside a special place for a shrine. Ask everyone to bring something to represent balance. This quiet place can also be used for meditation and contemplation.

Bring the group together to celebrate and focus the Five Elements. Set up each direction and its element, reflecting the abundance of the harvest in whatever way is appropriate to the space available.

Water in the West
Give thanks for the cleansing power of Water, washing away the dust of summer, bringing renewal and a new inner focus. Give thanks for the watery season about to begin as the rains replenish the Earth and sustain life. Give thanks for abundance of love and compassion, and deep connections. Give thanks for the gift of emotional expression. Through tears and laughter we are made full, helping us to find inner strength and helping us to move forwards.

Earth in the North
Give thanks for the harvest of the Earth and all her gifts of food, medicines, and all the resources we take. Give thanks for all the spirits of nature that now withdraw for rest and renewal. Give thanks for the wisdom we have gained through our experiences. These we now take within for understanding and assimilation. The physical harvest is a result of all our hard work and creativity. Celebrate what has been achieved and manifested.

Air in the East
Give thanks for communication, for new ideas and realisations. Give thanks for all the opportunities to share our thoughts and words with each other. Give thanks for the freedom of communication and the different methods of communication available. Give thanks for communications from beyond our world, for telepathy, for our inner voice. Resolve to balance these inner communication systems with the more acceptable outer forms.

Fire in the South

Give thanks for all the beneficial changes that have manifested. Celebrate your spontaneity and the strength of your will and courage. Celebrate your vitality and your health. If you are not well, give thanks and celebrate those days when you feel better. Celebrate and give thanks for your achievements and successes. Give thanks for your creativity. The active power of Fire now brings expansion and inner illumination and insights. Balance outer creative power with the spiritual journey within.

Spirit at the Centre

Give thanks for Spirit; within and without and ever present. We open our hearts to the abundance that this vital connection brings us. We give thanks for the power of Universal Love and connect to our source and the guidance from within. We reach out and touch the sacred, the still point of power at the centre of our being and through it we are at one.

The words I have written here are intended as clues and pathways to understanding. When invoking the elements, it is important to speak from the heart and with power, so that you help to make the connection strong for yourself and all those present. Use the elemental charts on pages 30-34 to help you.

Here at Autumn Equinox, the Earth's energy is balanced between the outer and the inner worlds. Now, at this point of balance, look back on what you have achieved and plant the seeds of where you wish to go. Share this with each other. Remember your seed vision of this moment by decorating and writing on a piece of card, birch bark or wood.

Focus on your feeling of balance and stillness and let sounds or notes out from deep within. Begin with a simple harmony of hums, and then let out any words that come to you. Whisper them, sing them, call them out! Help each other by echoing each other's words, notes, humming, droning, creating a rhythm of sound and movement. Weave together an expression of sound harmonising the power of the moment. Feel the power of expression as the unconscious and the conscious become balanced. Let yourself go, release your inhibitions, and celebrate your freedom to be yourself.

Go around the circle, each in turn, saying, "I love and approve of myself exactly the way I am." Go round several times until the energy shifts and begins to have power. Resolve to say this to yourself every day. It will bring great strength and healing.

Lie on the floor and, to a simple drumbeat, feel your breath become steady. Focus on the still point within. When you feel you are calm and connected to your inner being, ask for an image to help or guide you. Affirm that your spiritual path, respect for the Earth and each other, and love, will guide your actions. Make a drawing of your vision and any words that come to you and share it with each other afterwards.

Reflect on the gains and losses of the year. Give thanks for the outer expansion and what has been possible. Look at what is no longer needed, and what it is time to let go of with thanks and blessings, as you release the past.

Share with each other the seeds of your harvest that you take with you into the next cycle. Count your blessings. Celebrate your abundance.

Root Meditation
Plant your feet firmly on the ground, feet apart, and let your mind relax and come to rest in your lower abdomen, or hara. Let any tensions flow down through your body, and let your weight sink into the soles of your feet. Now begin to feel your roots reaching down into the Earth and spreading out like a tree's roots. Visualise the deep dark world within yourself and feel the contact with the Earth's energy as it flows through you, bringing calmness, nourishment and a strong firm foundation.

Using drums and percussion, dance your harvest dance. Fill your heart with all that you have gained. Let out any sounds or words from within to express this. Echo each other's words to give them strength and power. Visualise the rays of the Sun being taken within, warming you from the inside. Celebrate yourself, balanced and whole.

Create a walking-meditation dance, with a few simple steps you can lose yourself in repeating. Centre your energy in the abdomen area or hara, as this will help you to stay grounded. Feel your feet firmly on the Earth and your energy returning to your roots way down deep under the Earth. Perhaps a simple chant will emerge.

Honour the dragon with a snake dance led by a dragon mask or dragon effigy. The dance begins with expansive expressive energy, with much noise, drumming, percussion, singing and celebration. Weave in and out and all around, and then into a wide circle. Gradually spiral the circle inwards until the energy begins to move within, quietly and slowly until the dragon is laid to sleep for the winter. All lie down and contemplate stillness, rest and renewal.

This is the time for reconciling opposites and bringing our whole selves into balance. Each light a candle for restored balance, and to help focus an area in your life that you feel needs balancing. Seek to balance light and dark, young and old, male and female, conscious and unconscious, emotion and detachment, active and passive, material and spiritual. Share with each other your new insights and understanding. Make some new intentions to focus on and incubate this winter.

Pass the talking stick or talking bowl around the circle. Let each say what each person feels grateful for and what has been learnt from the active phase.

Plant some native bulbs or tree seeds in pots to place outside. Plant your own inner seeds with them. Focus on your hopes, ideas, and intentions for the spring and your allegiance to the Earth. Plant some of the fruit, nuts, seeds and berries you have gathered for the Autumn Equinox, label them, leave them outside without saucers underneath, and see what comes up in the spring.

We all need to know we are loved and respected for who we are. Share what you value about each other. Celebrate and give thanks for your friendships. This too is part of your harvest. Pass the talking stick or talking bowl around several times.

Continue the process of letting go of things, ideas, conditioning, and values that are no longer serving you. Write them down on paper and burn them in the candle flame or fire as part of a ritual of letting go.

Blessing and giving thanks for the food you eat, creates a shift in awareness. Share with each other any blessings you know that can be said or sung before eating. Teach them to each other.

In the centre, place a Basket of Abundance into which everyone has put things they wish to give away, things they no longer need. Each lights a candle with thanks for their own harvest and abundance, and then takes something from the basket.

Come together for a closing ceremony. Thank the elements, the spirits of place, the spirit of Autumn Equinox, your spirit guides and helpers and each other. Sing one of the blessings songs you have learnt.

Bless the food and drink and have a great feast and celebratory party.

SAMHAIN

AUTUMN CROSS QUARTER FESTIVAL

End October/Beginning November

MID-SCORPIO ♏ FIXED WATER

Dark of the Moon

*Hallows Eve * Halloween*
All Souls Night

Feast of the Dead

Festival of Remembrance

The Ending and Beginning of the Celtic Year

SAMHAIN

Celtic understanding of the year's cycle saw death and darkness as important and necessary, and this part of the cycle as a period of rest and regeneration before rebirth. Samhain (pronounced Sow-ein), like Beltain, is a magical time. The veil between the seen world of matter and the unseen world of spirit becomes thin – a perceived crack in the fabric of space-time. It is a time for communication with the ancestors, a time for divination, omens, portents, and seeking to understand the inner mysteries. It is a time to drift, dream and vision, a time for inner journeys connecting to the wisdom within yourself.

THIS IS THE SUMMER'S END AND THE BEGINNING OF WINTER. It is the end and the beginning of the Celtic New Year, affirming rebirth in the midst of death and darkness. At Samhain, the Grain Mother becomes the Crone, the wise woman, the death aspect of her trinity, until she is reborn as her virgin aspect with the rebirth of the Sun at the Winter Solstice. The Sun king is sacrificed back into the land having swelled the seeds that now lie in the dark of the Earth until the Sun's return. He too becomes a death god and shaman, able to travel the inner realms. Samhain is named after an Aryan lord of death, Samana or Samavurt who, along with other pre-Christian male gods, was given the title the Grim Reaper, the Leveller, the Dark Lord, Leader of Ancestral Ghosts, the Judge of the Dead. Sata, the Great Serpent, was an underground aspect of the Sun found in ancient Egypt, the root of Satan, the Angel of Darkness. Pluto, Hades, Aidoneus, Saman, Sammael, Cronus, Saturn, Hermes, Samanik, were some of the old gods associated with death, and which the church personified as the devil. The church created hell out of the Celtic Underworld, and every sadistic cruel fantasy man could invent, was assigned to it. The Underworld and darkness became a place to fear and the Celtic understanding of its regenerative aspect became lost.

Hell was previously a Norse Queen of the Underworld, Hellenes, and 'Hel' was a uterine shrine, a sacred cave of rebirth deep within the Earth. The dark regenerative power of the goddess was honoured throughout the Celtic and ancient world. Rhea-Kronia (the female counterpart to Cronos) devoured time itself, returning to the dark elemental formless chaos before time. Kali or Kali Ma, the Dark Mother of the Hindu Triple Goddess, devoured her own children. Rhiannon, also known as the Mother of Time, also devoured her own children and rode her horse through the regions of the dark. Morgan le Fey, Morgan the Fate, Morrigan, the Queen of Phantoms, a death goddess, reappeared in the Arthurian legends as Morgan. Cerridwen who kept the Cauldron of Rebirth and Regeneration, was known as the Grandmother of Memory and the Keeper of the ancestral gateway. Cailleach, the Black Mother, made the world. Scotland was once Caledonia, the land given by Cailleach or Cale. 'Scotland' came from Scotia, a Roman goddess known as the Dark Aphrodite, and known to the Celts as Satha or Scythia. To the Scandinavians, she was known as Skadi, personified as an old woman, hag or Veiled One. Mana and Mara were ancient Roman Goddesses whose ancestral spirits were called Manes, and ruled the Underworld. Maia was the Greek grandmother of Magic, mother of Hermes, the enlightened one, who conducted the souls of the dead to the Underworld. Hecate was one of the oldest goddesses in her crone aspect, found in ancient Greece. She ruled Heaven, Earth, and the Underworld; she ruled magic, omens and prophecy and she was also known as Persephone, ruler of the Underworld of ancient myth. Other goddesses of the Underworld include Minerva, Athene, Sophia and Medusa. The word 'crone' may have come from Rhea Cronia, Old Mother Time, but may also be linked to 'corone', the carrion crow, which was sacred to the death goddesses. Black was the colour she assumed before her re-emergence as her white virgin aspect at the Winter Solstice. Samhain can be seen as a psychic return to the dark womb for regeneration and renewal.

In the Middle Ages, this dark aspect of the goddess became an object of fear. She became Queen of Witches, Queen of Ghosts, black, evil, capable of bad magic and all manner of diabolical doings. Hag originally meant holy woman, wise woman, healer. Old women were originally revered for their wisdom, as midwives and herbalists. But during the witch-hunt years, they were tortured and killed in the most sadistic ways by the church. It was obviously important to the church to destroy these women who had previously held such power and respect. We cannot undo all the centuries of persecution and debasement of women that the church brought to our land, but we can turn and acknowledge that it happened, try to understand it and work through our feelings about it. All over the world patriarchal religions have forced the female to retreat but, true to the natural cycles of regeneration in the dark, women are now re-emerging rejuvenated, made new, strengthened and changed.

The early shamanic traditions embraced both sexes. The Pagans and Druids did not exclude women, but recognised the differences between their energy, power and focus. These shamanic practices have never completely disappeared; they continue to change and develop. These practices included consulting the Runes, Tree Ogham, and other divinatory systems; scrying (seeing visions in clear water, mirrors or crystal balls); reading omens in the land, in clouds, in fire, from the appearance of animals or birds; clairvoyance; the interpretation of dreams and visions; necromancy (consultation with the ancestral dead); journeys to the Otherworld or inner world to seek a guardian, guide, ally, or power animal. Shamans and witches (the wise-women) were said to be able to shape-shift, to transform into the spirit shape of a totem animal and to travel the astral planes. This is not so far from the visualisations and spirit journeys many of us practise today.

Fear of magic brought about a great deal of superstition and the psychic arts became seen as demonic. Fear of punishment and even death further inhibited their progress, but also true to the cyclic nature of regeneration in the darkness, many of the old traditions are re-emerging now, rejuvenated by their period in the dark. They are being understood in new ways, reinterpreted in the light of a new age – true expressions of a living tradition.

Darkness was important to the Celts. To them it was as important as the light. Darkness and death had power that they did not fear. Here at Samhain, as the Earth is plunged into its darkest time of the year, they blessed the seeds whose germination in the dark would once again bring life when the Sun returned. They communicated with their ancestors, believing deceased family members could visit their loved ones at this time of the year when the veil between the worlds is thin. Places were laid at the table during the feast so that the recent dead could be with their families and friends. Both the word ghost and the word guest have their roots in the German 'geist', originally a spirit of the dead invited to the Samhain feast. Samhain became the Christian All Souls Night, All Hallows Eve (Halloween) of 31st October and All Souls Day of 1st November.

It was thought that others could also slip through the gap in space-time: the faerie, the sidhe, hobgoblins, elves and other mischief-makers. This is the root of Halloween's 'mischief night'. Later the emissaries of the devil were also feared along with evil ghosts and many 'horrors of hell', which were let loose on this night and which all good Christian folk were led to fear.

Bonfires called 'samhnagan' were lit on the hilltops – the tumuli and burial mounds of the community's past. All the other fires in the community were put out and were then rekindled from the samhnagan. Later, each village or household had their own bonfires. (Note the proximity to our bonfire night.) The church may have brought the people away from the burial mounds, but Samhain customs continued to thrive. In Wales, omens were read from white stones, which were thrown into the ashes of the fire and then interpreted the next morning by the marks found there. Halloween apple games grew out of the Celtic belief in the apple as a holy fruit, sacred and magical, a means to immortality, death and rebirth. The western paradise of Avalon, known as apple-land, was ruled by Morgan, Queen of the Dead. The fabled Isles of the western oceans, where the Greeks believed the golden apples of the Hesperides were to be found, also bestowed immortality. In Celtic myth, the apples of the goddess (sometimes called Hels apples, after the Underworld goddess Hellenes), signified a sacred marriage and a journey to the land of death and rebirth. Later, Hels apples became the poisoned apples of Christian folklore that the 'wicked witch' used to kill her victims. Cutting the apple transversely reveals the hidden five-pointed star in the core, the magic pentacle, sign of the dark mysteries of the goddess and protection. Apples continue to be used at Samhain for games and divination.

Womb and tomb were closely linked in the Celtic mind, and this explains why so many tombs of this period and earlier, had tunnel entrances leading to a dark inner chamber. Not only were they places where the important dead were buried, but also they are important centres of Earth energy that can be used to enhance inner journeying. This is the best time of year for this, for all inner exploration, for meditating and for connecting to the spirit realms whatever you perceive them to be.

213

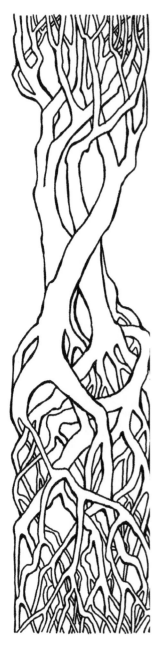

THE UNDERLYING ENERGY OF SAMHAIN

THIS IS THE CROSS QUARTER FESTIVAL OF AUTUMN'S END and the beginning of winter. Increasing darkness and cold means we must accept that winter is fast approaching and we must adjust to this changing season. Leaves have fallen off the trees, birds have migrated, animals have gone into hibernation, and frosts have come. It is a time of death and decay, death of the old, and within this, knowledge of rebirth. It is a time of forced adjustments that, once accepted, reveal a new set of possibilities, a new phase, a new power to life. It is the right time to connect to root energy and for internalising the creative life force. Like its counterpart Beltain, Samhain brings a mystical energy that we can use to explore and understand ourselves better.

This is the dark phase of the year's cycle when the mystery of transformation occurs. This process involves a descent and a death of something old in preparation for something new to be reborn. The descent into the Underworld or Otherworld can be understood as a journey into the unconscious and the spirit realms within each of us. Here we can find renewal through meditation, trance, rest, sleep, and by sacrificing our outer selves for a while. The seeds of our ideas and future direction in life are incubated in our unconscious during the winter months, ready for rebirth in the spring. We can honour the cycle by being aware that each end and death of the old will bring opportunity for a new start, as each beginning holds within it an end. This endless cycle of change is necessary, bringing renewal of cells, of our understanding, our ideas and ourselves. It means there are always new opportunities to start again, to stay healthy. Many illnesses are rooted in stuck energy patterns, emotional congestion and hanging on to the past.

We have been taught to fear our inner world and to mistrust the information we may receive through our intuition, and our connection to our own inherent inner wisdom. Many of our actions come from our subconscious thinking and belief patterns. We may not always be aware of the subtle conditioned responses that may silently rule our lives. We can use the energy of the dark time of the year to explore these inner parts of ourselves, to face our fear of the dark mysteries and magic and our deep unwanted feelings that we may have buried deep inside ourselves. We need to turn and face our fears with courage and determination and find the potential hidden within them. From this courageous journey will come transformation, a balanced perspective and rebirth in the age-old tradition of Samhain.

Use this time for inner exploration, astral travel, deep meditation, contacting your deepest wisdom. Slip beyond the rational and the logical. Explore the wild edges of yourself, beyond the seen and the known and the safe. Fear is one of our greatest teachers. Turn and look at what you fear and where the roots of this may lie. By being open to your intuition and wise-self, new insights and realisations may be revealed. Use this time of rest to seek out the old patterns of thought or behaviour that are not serving you well. Once revealed you can choose to think and live in a different way.

Review and assimilate what you have learned in the active phase of the year's cycle. Out of a difficult situation comes power, hope, clarity, rebirth, inner strength, wisdom and maturity. Use this time for learning, for collecting, sorting and memorising information, so that when the time for action comes, you will have assimilated new knowledge that can be used when needed. Nurture new visions, dreams, ideas and direction. Let them incubate in the dark winter months ready for when the active phase begins again.

I am tomorrows ancestor
The future of yesterday
and what I am in the here and now
goes rippling out all ways
Goes rippling out
always.

You are tomorrows ancestor
The future of yesterday
and what you are in the here and now
goes rippling out all ways
Goes rippling out
always.

We are tomorrows ancestor
The future of yesterday
and what we are in the here and now
goes rippling out all ways
Goes rippling out
always.

Brian Boothby
Tomorrows Ancestor

PREPARATIONS FOR SAMHAIN

*Burial Mounds * Astral Travel * Scrying*
*Seeing Auras * Crystal Allies * Divination/Omens/Portents*
*Power Animals * The Pentacle * Persephone*
*The Cauldron of Regeneration * Masks*
*Tree Planting and Coppicing * Reclaiming the Witch*
*Shamanic Journeying * Besom Broom*
*Trees: Elder * Yew*
*Herbs: Dandelion Root * Mugwort * Valerian * Elderberry*

Use the power of the Dark Moon to enhance your Samhain celebrations.

Prepare to have a large bonfire if you have got an outdoor space big enough. It is cold at this time of year, so the fire is important for warmth as well as focus. If you are celebrating with friends, ask everyone to bring wood for the fire and food to share. Create an area where people can put their wood when they arrive, and some tables where food can be put. Have an alternative plan for inside celebrating in case it rains. If possible, arrange to seat everyone for the Samhain feast. Buy lots of candles.

Create an outside shrine area by erecting a dolmen from three flat stones. The uprights will need to be embedded in the ground. You can add a fourth stone at the back. It may be small enough to put a candle in or as large as you can physically manage. Finding the flat stones will determine the size.

Alternatively, erect a standing stone in your garden or on your land where you feel the Earth's energy is strong, where you like to sit, where meditation comes easy. Choose a stone that has a good energy and embed it well into the Earth. Plant crystals beneath it, as well as all your good intentions and thanks for the Earth.

Make time to go to the long barrows, burial mounds or tumuli in your area. These can be found on any ordnance survey map. They are often to be found in the high places connecting and linking the ley alignments and the old dragon paths. In the Irish tradition, the barrows were called 'the hollow hills', said to be built by the sidhe so that mortals could enter fairyland. The same folklore reoccurs throughout Europe. Hidden in folk stories is reference to their use as gateways into another world, as places where people could communicate with the dead, journey to other lands where time stood still. Their acoustic properties are particularly interesting and worth exploring. They have an extraordinary atmosphere that will challenge and transform you through your experiences there.

Inner Journeying

Now is a good time for inner journeys and developing your psychic skills. Astral travel is best practised with a friend. Take it in turns to sit with each other and talk through the procedure. Be there for each other after the journey, and for assurance while journeying. Lie down comfortably and breathe deeply and calmly, focusing on the centre of your body. Feel yourself getting smaller and smaller until you are tiny. Then feel yourself getting bigger and bigger until you fill the whole room. Repeat this again, and then feel yourself normal size but floating above your body. See the golden thread which connects your spirit self to your body. Know with certainty that this cannot be broken in any way. When you feel ready, calmly allow yourself to float away above the room, the house, over town and countryside, moving further away until you are in space above the Earth. Look around and see if there is a guide who might speak to you or show you something, like a symbol, a vision, or a series of events like in a dream. When you feel ready to return to your body, thank your guide and gently journey back through the stars to the Earth, back the way you came to the room you are in, and come gently back into your body. Wiggle your toes and fingers, stretch yourself and take time to feel properly back before sitting up and recalling your experience. Write down or record all the details now, and look at interpreting their meanings later. It is important to do this straight away while the experience is fresh in your mind. Eat and drink afterwards to help settle yourself fully back in your body. Look for what understanding you have gained and write this down too.

Scrying

This is another skill associated with this time. Light some candles and state your intention. Fill a dark glass bowl with mineral water. Focus on your breath as you would for meditation, and gaze at the surface of the water. Half close your eyes and let them glaze out of focus. Stay relaxed and breathe slowly and deeply. You may find you slip out of normal time and become aware of seeing images in the mind or on the surface of the water. Scrying can also be done outside under the Full Moon, using the Moon's light to help images for form and flow.

Divination, Omens, and Portents

The Celts used this time to seek omens and portents. They would consult the ancestors and look for signs from the natural world. They cast the knucklebones, runes, or ogham sticks. All the divinatory systems involve random throwing or random choosing from a system of symbols, each with many layers of meaning. The process of interpreting them was called 'raedan' or reading. The result was raedels or riddles as the results had to be interpreted by the reader or seer.

Make your own runes or ogham sticks, so that you can take your time to learn the meanings behind each one as you make them. Choose your material and carve each rune symbol in turn on to pieces of slate, bone, wood, or clay. (The clay will then need to be fired.) Similarly with the Celtic Tree Ogham, each stick is collected after direct communication with each tree, and the ogham symbol is carved, painted or drawn onto the wood. They are used as aids to understanding the tree's wisdom and inherent energy. Make a pouch to keep them in, and keep a journal of your readings, with a note of the date. Winter is a good time to study and learn to use any of these systems. Having assimilated information in the unconscious, it can be accessed by the conscious mind in creative and inspirational ways.

Reflect on the visions that have been living on the edge of your consciousness. Make visible the invisible. Take up drawing or painting and let your unconscious speak to you through the images you produce. It doesn't matter whether you can draw or paint in the conventional sense. Let your notions of what is 'good' go, and seek the seeds of your inner world as you see what is revealed. Your 'technique' will improve the more you do, as will your confidence.

Reclaiming the Witch

There is still a great need to undo the negative propaganda surrounding the old witch woman. The Crone aspect of the Triple Goddess was once respected for being the most powerful phase of a woman's life under the matriarchal tribal system, but it became the most feared by the patriarchal church. To the ancients this third, post-menopausal stage of a woman's life was her wisest, as she retained her wise Moon blood and, of course, the whole tribe could benefit from her wisdom gained over the years. The word 'witch' is derived from the Anglo-Saxon 'witan' meaning 'to see', to know, and a 'witea' was a seer or diviner, becoming 'wicca' (masculine seer, wise man) and 'wicce' (female seer, wise woman). The 'Witch' became a convenient scapegoat for any natural disaster, disease, crop failure, or petty rivalry. Family fortunes which previously were passed down through the female line, could immediately be seized by the church, and any woman who made trouble or was too powerful or influential, could be charged with witchcraft, tortured until 'confession' and sadistically killed. It is an appalling history. Supported by Christianised folktales, witch became synonymous with evil, black, bad magic, ugly old women, and fear. Now we no longer fear old women, but we rarely honour them either. The evil witch is still more likely to be part of children's stories than a good witch capable of wondrous magical transformations and great wisdom. Change the old stories, or find new stories and read them to the children. Help reverse the old images and generate respect for the power of the old ones, and the power of transformation.

Who can walk on their own at night? Who can walk alone in the dark woods, or sit alone in the dark by a sacred spring or burial mound? Who sees power in black but not evil? What does magic mean to you? Unravel what is true for you and what you fear. Turn and face the fear. Release its hold over you.

Contemplate and review your year which has ended, and look what gifts life has bought you this year. Look for old mental and emotional attitudes that no longer make you happy or ring true for you and make a decision to move on from them. Transform the things that are holding you back or no longer serve your higher good. Let them go and move on with freedom. Let your heart decide and guide your actions. Regeneration, rebirth and transformation are constantly yours.

Power Animals

There are many power animals and birds associated with Samhain, and a witch or shaman's ability to shape-shift into the guise of an animal or bird was greatly feared. Ravens, crows, blackbirds, owls, eagles, bats, cats – were all seen as familiars (spirit friends) of witches and shamans. The horse was associated with the dark goddess Rhiannon, and in folklore the horse always knew the way into the Otherworld and was often a guide and companion there. Birds were thought to travel freely between the worlds and were seen as messengers. Ravens were thought of as oracular birds bringing omens and foretelling the future. Owls were known for their wisdom. The Romans called the owl 'strix', the same word they used for 'witch'. The owl was also called

Night Hag and was feared as an emissary of the witch. Crows and vultures took the souls of the dead to the Otherworld and storks brought them back. The eagle is known for transformation and rebirth. Blackbirds were said to enchant people with their song, especially at twilight, leading them into Faerie and the lands outside of time that co-exist with ours. Faeries could change into birds, which is why they are depicted with wings.

The Pentacle

This is the Star of Knowledge, the star of life and health; it was used by Hermetic magicians to represent Man the Microcosm. The head, arms, and feet of a man within a pentacle touched a circle at the five points, with his genitals at the exact centre (the shape of woman as well, of course!). The point of a pentacle should always be at the top. The five-pointed star in a circle was the Egyptian hieroglyph for the underground womb of transformation. Cutting an apple transversely reveals the five-pointed star inside. The small twigs of the English oak tree (the sacred tree of the Druids) reveals a perfect five-pointed star running through their centre. It represents the Five Elements: Earth, Air, Fire, Water with Spirit at the top. The drawing of a pentacle as a single unbroken line can be used as a force field, a protection from unwanted influences or intrusion. Because of its magical associations with the old religion, in the church's eyes it became associated with the devil, the witch's cross, and with evil.

Persephone

Persephone was the daughter of Demeter, the Corn Mother who, in classical Greek myth, was abducted by a male god Pluto and taken into the Underworld. The Earth became perpetually winter until he agreed to release her in the spring, but only if she returned to him again in the autumn. This is a later reworking of an older story of Persephone, a dark goddess, who descended into the Underworld for regeneration and rebirth. Pluto was also an earlier dark goddess, a daughter of the Cretan Earth Mother Rhea, one of the Titans or older deities. Later, Pluto became masculinised and, along with other gods and goddesses of the Underworld, became synonymous with the church's idea of the devil.

The Cauldron of Regeneration and the Holy Grail

In all the early traditions there is a vessel, chalice or cauldron that held the secret of life and death, the mysteries, the power of healing, transformation and rebirth. The Cauldron of Regeneration was central to Celtic spiritual understanding of death and rebirth as the never-ending cycle of life. It appears over and over again in the folktales and legends of the Celtic lands. The year's solar cycle provides each of us with an experience of death and rebirth through a period of rest during the winter months. This is a time of reconnection to inner wisdom and the mysteries accessed through the unconscious realms, before the rebirth of the Sun heralds the return of the active phase of a new year at Winter Solstice. Later, the Cauldron of Regeneration was assimilated into Arthurian legend as the Holy Grail sought by the knights of the round table who looked for ways to re-interpret the old knowledge and the ways of the goddess through the new religion of Christianity.

Masks

Traditionally worn at Samhain and used in magic since earliest times. Northern shamans believed they could put on a 'Helkappe' or Hel-met (a mask of the goddess Hellenes) which would make them invisible and help them enter the Otherworld. This same shaman's mask appeared in medieval mystery plays as the mask of Death worn by Hades, the Grim Reaper, Lord of Death, as he performed his 'dance macabre'. Masks were worn in shamanic trance-work where death and rebirth were part of transformative rites of passage. The mask can be seen to 'possess' the wearer, allowing the person behind the mask to take on a different identity. Magical masks will bring power and spirit that must not be underestimated. When used in a ceremony, they may release an energy source within the wearer, or access deep hidden parts of themselves. Masks have been worn at Halloween as part of the fun of disguise and trickery, but they hold a deeper power if used wisely and with respect. Masks may be used as part of a rite of passage; as an act of transformation; for expressing an archetype; to invoke a totem power animal or bird spirit. (Making Masks see pages 47 and 48.)

Making a Besom Broom

Birch is associated with purification and renewal. Birch twigs were used to drive out the spirits of the old year, re-establish tribal boundaries (beating the bounds) and drive out malevolent spirits. Birch twigs are cut now to make besom brooms for sweeping up the old year's leaves. Gather a large bunch of birch twigs and tie them together tightly at the thick end of the twigs. Cut a hazel or ash broom handle, sharpen one end, and drive it into the middle of the bundle. Seen as the 'witch's broom' of folk stories, you could indeed use it as a broom for symbolic work, making clean sweeps, clearing energy and creating boundaries.

TREES OF SAMHAIN

ELDER – *Sambucus nigra*

The fifteenth tree of the Celtic Tree Ogham: RUIS. R. Elder is known as a tree of regeneration and wisdom. Elder will help move stuck emotional states, moving the energy from the surface levels to bring deeper understanding. Often called the witch's tree, the Elder Mother, the Queen of Trees, it is connected to the Triple Goddess and the crone energy, in particular. There are many strong superstitions about cutting the elder, and especially about bringing it into the house and burning it. This included fear of releasing a malevolent spirit from within it. There is good reason for this, because when it burns it releases cyanide. It is best to put any fallen wood in the habitat pile in a corner and let nature claim its own. With so many herbal and culinary uses, it is better to let these beautiful trees grow freely. Make the most of their seasonal gifts and give your thanks to the tree if you are blessed to have one near you. Elder makes a fast-growing hedge, easily propagated by pushing small pieces of freshly cut twigs into the ground.

Elder is a tree of endings and beginnings. As the old year ends, potential for new beginnings are revealed. Each end brings a new beginning; each beginning contains within it, its end. Elder is known as the tree of regeneration, renewal and transformation; it brings wisdom to help deal with changes. In early times elder was used to bless a person, place or object. Its branches were hung in doorways of houses, cowsheds; its leaves were buried in graves and its twigs carried to ward off evil. At Samhain, the last of the elderberries were picked with solemn rites. The wine made from these berries was considered to be the last sacred gift of the Earth goddess, and was highly valued and drunk ritually to invoke prophecy and divination.

Elderberries help to throw off congestion and boost the immune system, helping to ward off colds. Elderberry wine has curative powers of established repute. Taken hot at night, it will help in the early stages of a cold or flu and is excellent for sore throats and catarrh. This is due to the viburnic acid contained in the berries that induces perspiration and helps bring the cold out. An old cure for colds, coughs and bronchitis, was to make a rob (a juice thickened by heat) of elderberries. Use five pounds of fresh ripe berries plucking them off the stalks with a fork. Crush with one pound of sugar and boil until it is the thickness of honey. One or two tablespoons mixed with hot water at night will act as a demulcent to the chest and throat.

YEW – *Taxus baccata*

Yew is the last tree of the Celtic Tree Ogham: IDHADH or IDHO. I. Like Samhain, it represents the end of one cycle and the beginning of a new one. All races of the Northern Hemisphere have a deep respect for this remarkable tree that survived from the Ice Age. A new system of dating now suggests that some of the old English yews are thousands of years old due to their ability to grow a new trunk from the decaying mass of the old trunk, keeping their original root bole. The yew is associated with immortality, renewal, regeneration, everlasting life, rebirth, transformation and access to the Otherworld and the ancestors. Known as the death tree, the whole tree is poisonous, apart from the fleshy part of the fruit. Sacred to Hecate and the Crone aspect of the Triple Goddess, the wood was prized for sacred carving and votive offerings. If you carve this beautiful wood, be aware that the dust produced by sanding, is poisonous. Spending time with the yew will help overcome fear of endings. We may fear death, or the death of our old selves or an old way of life, but each death can be seen as a new beginning, as hope for the future, and transformation. Sometimes one thing needs to end before something new can begin.

Tree Planting and Coppicing

The winter months, from November to early March, is the best time for planting trees and moving saplings, bushes, or splitting herbs. If you have land, you might want to plant a Celtic Tree Circle (see page 58) or create a new grove of trees for celebration and ritual. It is also the right time for coppicing (cutting a tree right back to the bole at the base of the trunk). This encourages the tree to send up many long straight poles instead of just one central trunk. Most native trees can be coppiced (not birch or pine), to give a variety of straight poles for domestic use. November to March is also the traditional time for cutting willow whips for basket-making, and hazel poles for hurdle-making, when the sap is down and the leaves are off the trees. Hazel poles can be used for making garden screens, creative fencing, archways and garden bowers.

HERBS OF SAMHAIN

DANDELION ROOT – *Taraxacum officinale*
Dig up the roots from November to March. If you wish to dry and store them, wash them and scrub gently, but do not leave to soak. Chop them up and leave them to dry in brown paper bags in a warm airy place until brittle. Store them in a dark jar. Take a tablespoon of the chopped root and leave overnight in a glass of cold water. Put in a saucepan (not aluminium) with more water, bring to the boil and simmer for ten minutes. When cool, pour the unstrained liquid into a jug and store covered in the fridge. Drink one wineglassful three times a day. This is a prime lymph tonic, removing poisons from the system and cleansing the blood. Use for any disturbances of the liver. It is a useful herb for emotional stagnation, turning depression into expression and self-empowerment. (Similarly with the leaves.)

MUGWORT – *Artemisia vulgaris*
This is often to be found growing on waste grounds, besides footpaths and along roadsides and was one of the nine sacred herbs of ancient times. It is a powerful blood cleanser and general tonic that stimulates the action of the liver. It is an antiseptic, relaxant and astringent. Taken hot, it will bring on a delayed period, and help with painful periods. Mugwort has a long history of magical and ritual uses, enhancing clairvoyance, astral travel and dream work. It can be burnt as an incense or drunk as a herb tea.

N.B. Do not use if pregnant.

VALERIAN – *Valeriana officinalis*
The roots are a powerful painkiller and are also used for any condition that needs the whole system to relax. It will relieve anxieties and digestive upsets brought about by stress. It brings courage and a calm mind. It is a prime remedy for insomnia caused by an overactive or troubled mind. Use for grounding someone who has become overwhelmed by physical trauma, terror or fear. Dig the plant in the autumn or spring, chop off the white roots and replant the plant. Make into a tincture or dry and use as a cold infusion as its taste is very strong.

N.B. Do not take when driving.

SAMHAIN CELEBRATIONS

These are some suggestions for celebrating Samhain.

Samhain embraces the power of the dark and is celebrated as part of the Dark Moon cycle. You may wish to be inside for some of the time, lighting the fire at a beginning or the end of the celebration. Get the fire ready to light beforehand and cover with a piece of plastic if it looks like rain. Have plenty of dry kindling ready to add at the last minute.

Make a shrine to celebrate Samhain. Hang up black, brown and purple cloths and ribbons. Gather sprays of dried grasses, herbs, twigs, baskets of apples, haws, rose hips, sloes. Ask everyone who is coming to celebrate to bring something for the shrine that is powerful to them and reflects the energy of Samhain, including photos of loved ones who have died. Light the shrine well with candles; candle lanterns or night lights in jam jars. If you are celebrating on your own, the creation of this sacred shrine on a shelf, table or window ledge is a powerful connection to your Samhain celebration.

Make yourself a Samhain headdress, weaving plants and natural things from the old year. Use ivy, honeysuckle or old man's beard as a base, adding herbs, sprays of berries, dried grasses, the last flowers.

Make a representation or effigy of the old year using similar things. Place this in a central position to honour the old year passing. Each person makes a spray or posy to honour the year for themselves and adds it on, saying what moves them.

Gather in a circle to a gentle drumbeat. If you are on your own drum for a while, focus your energy. Place something in each of the directions around your central shrine and give thanks for each element in turn.

Water in the West
We give thanks for the element of Water for the rain and the replenishment of the Earth that it brings. We give thanks for all the underground water of the land, for the life-giving springs of the land. We acknowledge and give thanks for the ending of cycles, for the deep parts of ourselves, and the mystical side of life, which opens us to other parts of ourselves. Water connects us to our intuition, and inner wisdom. It helps us to be receptive and open to the flow of our deep knowing. May we find inner purpose and freedom to follow our hearts.

Earth in the North
We give thanks to the Earth for all its gifts of food and shelter, which we take with us now into the winter. We give thanks for the ending of the cycle and all it has given us. We give thanks for the dark days and the opportunity to rest now and for the inner nourishment this will bring. Blessings on the seeds that lie dormant in the dark Earth until the spring. Blessings on the root energy now beginning. May our own roots grow strong and bring us inner stability.

Air in the East
We give thanks for the element of Air and our ability to communicate on many levels. May we keep open to new thoughts, messages from our intuitive selves, the birth of new ideas and inspiration from within. May we speak out our truth and let our voices carry our visions through our words, songs and invocations. May all the good and positive things that inspire us travel out into the world to make a difference.

Fire in the South
We give thanks for the element of Fire, the active power of the will and the creativity that we take with us now into the dark cycle. We make use of its power to transform and cleanse, and we fire up our passion to learn and assimilate. We give thanks for our inner Fire that brings strength of purpose, courage and spontaneity, and the burning away of old outworn patterns.

Spirit at the Centre
We give thanks to Spirit, for the stabilising influence it brings into our lives. It cannot be seen and it cannot be named and yet it is part of all of us. Here in the dark time of the year we celebrate our inner connection and welcome the guidance from our ancestors, the angels and our guardians in the spirit world. We welcome the chance to rest in the dark, in the still clear place of unconditional love and compassion.

The words I have written here are intended as clues and pathways to understanding. When invoking the elements, it is important to speak from the heart and with power, so that you help to make the connection strong for yourself and all those present. Use the elemental charts on pages 30-34 to help you.

Create a circle of power and protection around you, and all those gathered. State with firm intent that the circle is a protective force field and picture an energy of light around the circle. Light candles at the four directions and in the centre. Welcome the guardians and spirit helpers of all present into your circle.

In the centre of the circle, place a bowl of sand and let each person light a candle with thanks for the old year. This is a reflective quiet time, a time to stare into the flames and connect to your inner self.

Honour and name those who have died who have influenced you. Share the lessons and wisdom you have gained from them. Light a candle for family and friends who have died, honour them and welcome them into your heart. Do not try to call them back in any way, as this could interfere with their own journey.

Pass around a bag of small crystals and let each person take one, asking for its help and guidance through the winter months. Spend time holding your crystal and being open to receiving guidance and inspiration.

Release into the fire or flames what is holding you back: insecurities, fear of failure, fear of not being loved, old mental and emotional attitudes, old ways of behaving, lack of trust, lack of confidence. Leave it behind in the old year. Write these down on pieces of paper or strips of silver birch bark. Let each say, "I leave behind..." and at the same time give the pieces of paper or birch bark to the flames to transform.

Leaving behind these things will make room for new beginnings, new plans, new ways of being. Let each say what new seeds they will incubate through the winter months, to manifest in the next growth cycle. Have a dish of freshly picked acorns for this. Let each say, "I plant the seed of..." and take an acorn or two to plant.

Pass round a bowl of garden-picked apples. Cut your apple around the middle to reveal the five-pointed star within. Each seed can be seen as a new beginning in your life. Chew each seed thoroughly to take its energy within and name what the seeds mean to you.

Shamanic Journeying

Use this time to journey to the Otherworld to meet a guardian, spirit guide or power animal. The sound of a steady drumbeat will greatly enhance an inner journey. If you are on your own, this could be recorded or found on CDs made for this purpose. A rapid drumbeat is the signal to return to your body. Begin with a little ceremony, like lighting a candle, some incense, and make an invocation of intent. Lie down with a blanket over you and breathe deeply and steadily. Close your eyes and drift away from physical reality, feeling completely safe and relaxed. Visualise in your mind a beautiful place in nature. When that place is strong and detailed, look around for a hole in the ground, in a tree trunk, or a tunnel, an opening that goes deep deep down into the Earth. Enter this hole and journey down it for as long as you need to, until the scenery changes and you find yourself in another place. Look around you and be open to meet your ally, spirit guide, guardian or power animal that is here to help you. Observe what you see here, any visions that may be given to you, symbols or feelings. When you feel ready, thank the spirit ally for its help and return up the tunnel into the natural world you first visualised. Relax here a while and then return to your physical body the way you came. Once awareness of the room in which you lay returns, wiggle your toes and fingers, and open your eyes. Write down what happened on your journey and what you understand. If you are with others, share what has been revealed.

Share with each other what you have learnt from the old year and where this understanding brings you. Look for the direction this will lead you to, how this will serve your greater good and the greater good of the Earth.

Honour the cycle of death and rebirth. Honour grief and loss. Honour friends and family who have died. Honour death as part of life.

Put on your Samhain mask and dance a dance of the year's end. Drumbeat will enhance this. Let go of your fears and your inhibitions. Let out any cries or sounds you want to make. End the dance by returning to earth to rest and regenerate in the dark.

Make a labyrinth. (See page 134.) Light it with night-lights in jam jars. Chant and drum as you support each other to walk its ancient pattern. Seek guidance from the still point at the centre. Write down any revelations or insights when you come out.

Tell stories which celebrate the shaman, the witch and the Crone, and which reflect their ancient understanding, tales of Otherworld, inner journeying and transformation. Storytelling would have been an integral part of any tribe or family gathering in the past, especially through the long dark nights of winter. Rekindle this ability by asking everyone to bring a story, to tell in their own words. A story that is repeated regularly becomes rich with inner understanding on many levels. Discuss its deeper meanings; make adjustments; strengthen it each time it is told.

Light the Samhain fire with ceremony and invocation. Use the power of Fire to transform, cleanse and purify. Use sticks (sweet-smelling apple wood prunings are wonderful) or birch bark, to focus what you wish to leave behind in the old year and offer it to the flames to transform. Symbolically burn what you wish to be finished with, perhaps an old way of life, old habits, patterns, and old ways of thinking that you wish to change. Give to the flames what is holding you back. Do what you need to do. Then Fire up what you wish to transform in yourself and incubate in the winter months. Tap into your passion, your deep longings that live deep within your being. By empowering your self you set things in motion and create change for the future.

Place the effigy of the old year somewhere it can disintegrate and return to earth. With ceremony, let the old year go with thanks for all its gifts. Give thanks for all you have learnt, for friendships, for all that you manifested for yourself, for all the opportunities, experiences and love it brought. Let it all go now so that you are free to begin a new cycle. Maybe something will grow here in the spring from the berries or seed heads you used.

Choose three cards from the Tarot pack, three Runes, or three Ogham sticks. The first choice represents the Underworld aspect, giving guidance to the root of a situation, something from the past, or something hidden. The second choice is laid above the first and it represents the material world, the present moment caught in time. Interpret it in the light of the first. It also represents your manifest power, your physical, mental, emotional and spiritual situation at the present moment. The third choice is the most fluid and reflects the Otherworld aspect. This is the realm where all possibilities exist and will provide you with insights into the direction you are flowing towards. Choose the most spiritual and positive interpretation. Trust your most immediate impressions and insights. Give your intuition a chance to guide your thoughts.

Bring everyone together for the closing circle. Hold hands and together thank each of the elements for their energy. Thank the spirits of place, your spirit guides and helpers, the ancestors and descendants. End on a meditative chant.

Bless the food and drink and have a feast. In the old tradition of Samhain, leave a space and food at the feast for family and friends who have recently died.

ABOUT THE AUTHOR

GLENNIE KINDRED IS A MUCH-LOVED TEACHER OF NATURAL LORE, celebrating the Earth's cycles, creating ceremony, native trees and native plant medicine, and alchemy. She has a strong and committed following and enjoys sharing her insights through a wide range of popular workshops and talks, and through her books. She encourages and inspires people to open their hearts to the interconnection of all of life and wonder for the Earth, and to create and co-create simple ceremony as a tool for transformation and heartfelt connection. She is renowned for her ability to enthuse people with a love for life, and the power that we can individually and collectively create to bring about positive change, both for ourselves and for the Earth.

She lives on the edge of a small market town in Derbyshire with her partner Brian Boothby, where she enjoys gardening, growing native plants and trees, kitchen medicine, many creative projects, celebrating the Earth's cycles, her friends and family and her local community. She is active in the Transition Towns' initiative. Her passions include her family, walking the land barefoot, guerrilla gardening, travelling, and being alive to the wonders and delights of the natural world. She has three adult children, May, Jack and Jerry and a granddaughter, Evie Rose.

GLENNIE KINDRED is the author of eleven books on Earth wisdom, celebrating the Earth's cycles, creating ceremony, the elements, herbal healers, hedgerow foraging, native plants and native trees, the tree ogham, kitchen medicine and alchemy. To buy her books, postcards, limited edition prints of some of her pen and ink drawings, as well as her workshop and talks calendar, her magazine articles, and monthly native plants and trees pages, please visit:

www.glenniekindred.co.uk

OTHER BOOKS BY GLENNIE KINDRED

Earth Cycles of Celebration, 1991, revised 2002 and 2013.
Sacred Tree, 1995, revised 2003.
The Tree Ogham, 1997.
Creating Ceremony,with Lu Garner, 2002.
Elements of Change, 2009.
Herbal Healers, Wooden Books, 1999, revised 2002.
Hedgerow Cookbook, Wooden Books, 1999, revised 2002.
Earth Wisdom, Hay Hous,. First published 2004, revised 2011.
Earth Alchemy, Hay House, 2013. (First Published as *The Alchemists Journey*, 2005.)
Letting In the Wild Edges, Permanent Publications, 2013.

All books available direct from Glennie's website, signed and dedicated on request:

www.glenniekindred.co.uk

The Earth Pathways Diary

Glennie is the co-founder and editor of the *Earth Pathways Diary*; It includes the Moon phases and signs for the year and the sunrise and sunset times, moonrise and moonset times and some astrological information for the UK; and includes a focus for each of the Earth Festivals throughout the Wheel of the Year. There is a page-a-week view, month-at-a-view planners, a year planner and notes pages.

The Earth Pathways diary celebrates the work of UK artists and writers who share a deep love for our land and a vision of a sustainable future for all. More than just a diary, it is a networking resource and inspiration for the growing community of people who are willing to actively create positive change in their lives for the benefit of the Earth.

To contribute to the diary or buy:

www.earthpathwaysdiary.co.uk

RECOMMENDED READING

It is impossible to list all the sources that have influenced me over the years. Information becomes assimilated and ideas form, reform and move on. Much of this book has grown out of my own intuitive understanding and experience working with the eight Celtic festivals by myself and with groups over many years. It therefore includes much unique material and ideas. I would, however, like to thank the following books for their information and inspiration at the time of reading:

Aburrow, Yvonne; *The Enchanted Forest,* Capall Bann Publishing, 1994.

Aburrow, Yvonne; *Sacred Grove,* Capall Bann Publishing, 1994.

Andrews, Lynn; *The Power Deck,* Harper San Francisco, 1991.

Aziz, Peter; *Working with Tree Spirits in Shamanic Healing,* Points Press, 1994.

Brooke, Elizabeth; *A Woman's Book of Herbs,* The Women's Press, 1992.

Burl, Aubrey; *A Guide to the Stone Circles of Britain,* Ireland and Brittany, Yale University Press, 1995.

Capra, Fritjof; *The Tao of Physics,* Fontana/Collins, 1982.

Carey, Diana and Large, Judy; *Festivals, Family and Food,* Hawthorn Press, 1982.

Cooper, Stephanie, Fynes-Clinton and Rowling, Marye; *The Children's Year,* Hawthorn Press, 1986.

Davis, Courtney; *The Celtic Art Source Book,* Blandford, 1988.

Davis, Courtney; *The Art of Celtica,* Blandford, 1994.

Estes, Clarissa Pinkola; *Women who run with the Wolves,* Rider, 1992.

Frazer, James George; *The Golden Bough,* Macmillan London, 1949.

Glickman, Michael; *Corn Circles,* Wooden Books, 1996.

Graves, Robert; *The White Goddess,* Faber and Faber, 1990.

Grieve, Mrs M; *A Modern Herbal,* Tiger Books International, 1994.

Gurudas; *The Spiritual Properties of Herbs,* Cassandra Press, 1988.

Hay, Louise; *You can Heal your Life,* Hay House, 1986.

Hoffman, David; *The Holistic Herbal,* Findhorn Press, 1983.

Hoult, Janet; *Dragons,* Gothic Image Publications, 1985.

Martineau, John; *Mazes and Labyrinths in Great Britain,* Wooden Books, 1996.

Matthews, John; *The Celtic Shaman,* Element Books, 1991.

Meadows, Kenneth; *Earth Medicine,* Element Books, 1989.

Meadows, Kenneth; *The Medicine Way,* Element Books, 1990.

Michell, John; *The New View Over Atlantis,* Thames and Hudson, 1983.

Noyes, Ralph; *The Crop Circle Enigma,* Gateway Books, 1990.

Purce, Jill; *The Mystic Spiral,* Thames and Hudson, 1987.

Scheffer, Mechthild; *Bach Flower Therapy,* Thorsons, 1990.

Service, Alastair and Bradbery, Jean; *The Standing Stones of Europe,* Weidenfeld and Nicolson, 1996.

Thorsson, Edred; *The Book of Ogham,* Llewellyn, 1994.

Walker, Barbara. G; *The Women's Encyclopaedia of Myths and Secrets,* Harper and Row, 1983.

White Eagle; Spiritual Unfoldment, White Eagle Publishing Trust, 1992.

The Dragon Project; Circles of Silence, Don Robins, Souvenir Press, London, 1985.

INDEX

with thanks

With this new revised edition of the old favourite
Sacred Celebrations, I am thankful for this opportunity to
see it unfold into a new cycle as *Sacred Earth Celebrations*.

I also give heartfelt thanks to Maddy and Tim Harland of
Permanent Publications, for their support, care and determination
to rescue this book and to bring it into new life; to John Adams for
re-scanning all the artwork; to Sarah Howerd for the exciting new design
of the book, the cover design and for the enriching experience of
working creatively together; to Tony Rollinson for helping promote it;
to Marion McCartney for her proof reading and guidance; and to all those
who work behind the scenes, helping this book to travel far and wide.

With Love to those friends who contributed their poems and songs:
Brian Boothby, Vince DeCicco, and Nicki Martin, and to the loving
hearts of good friends who have helped and inspired me along the way;
to both the Celebrations Group and the Elementals; to the ancestors and
descendants, spirit guides and helpers who have opened the way; to my
lovely family who made space and time for me to write and draw when
I needed it; to the power and guidance of the Earth, the trees and plants
and this land to whom I give my allegiance.

Thank you all for your loving support

Enjoyed this book?
You might also like these
from Permanent Publications

The Biotime Log
Maddy Harland
£12.95
Beautifully illustrated,
you can note your
day-to-day nature
observations in this
ready-made book which
will last for years.

Walking With Trees
Glennie Kindred
£15.00
An intimate journey
describing the nature
of 13 native trees, our
relationship with them
and their relationship
with the web of life.

**Letting in
the Wild Edges**
Glennie Kindred
£14.95
How to grow and
manage native edible
and medicinal plants in
our gardens or on the
wild edges of the land.

Our titles cover:
permaculture, home and garden, green building,
food and drink, sustainable technology,
woodlands, community, wellbeing and so much more

Available from all good bookshops and online
retailers, including the publisher's online shop:

https://shop.permaculture.co.uk
with 10% off the RRP on all books

Our books are also available via our American distributor, Chelsea Green:
www.chelseagreen.com/publisher/permanent-publications

Permanent Publications also publishes *Permaculture Magazine*

Enjoyed this book?
Why not subscribe
to our magazine

Available as print and digital subscriptions, all with
FREE digital access to our complete 26 years of
back issues, plus bonus content

Each issue of *Permaculture Magazine* is hand crafted,
sharing practical, innovative solutions, money saving
ideas and global perspectives from a grassroots
movement in over 170 countries

To subscribe visit:

www.permaculture.co.uk

or call 01730 823 311 (+441730 823 311)